ON

BALANCE

Was Britain a Net Gain for India?

MARK COLENUTT

The COMMONWEALTH
BRITISH

AUSTRALIA

METHINKS I SEE IN MY MIND A
NOBLE AND PUISSANT NATION
ROUSING HERSELF LIKE A STRONG
MAN AFTER SLEEP · AND
SHAKING HER INVINCI —
BLE LOCKS·

MILTON

OF NATIONS ~ OR ~ the EMPIRE

ONWARD

BRITAIN · I SEE HER IN HER OLD
AGE ~ BUT YOUNG · AND STILL
DARING TO BELIEVE IN HER POWER
OF ENDURANCE ~ WITH
STRENGTH STILL EQUAL
TO THE TIME

EMERSON

UNITATE

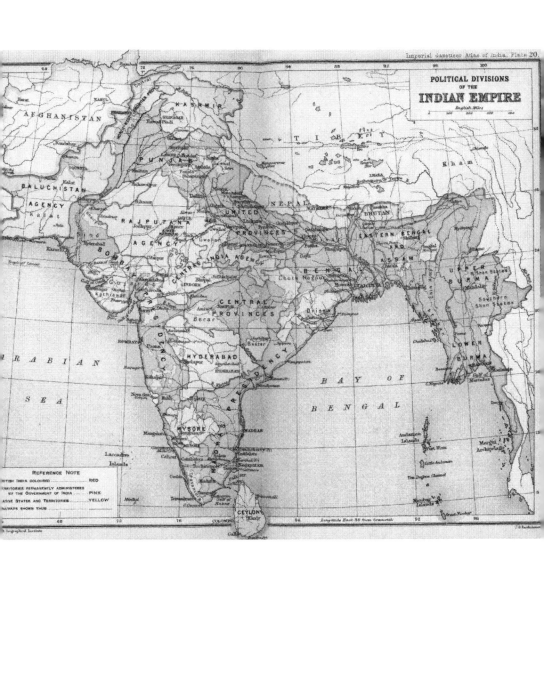

POLITICAL DIVISIONS
OF THE
INDIAN EMPIRE

English Miles

REFERENCE NOTE

BRITISH INDIA COLOURED .... RED
TERRITORIES PERMANENTLY ADMINISTERED
BY THE GOVERNMENT OF INDIA ..... PINK
NATIVE STATES AND TERRITORIES ... YELLOW
RAILWAYS SHOWN THUS

I would like to take this opportunity to thank my wife, Daniela, without whose patience and continuing support throughout my research and writing, this work could never have been completed. A special thanks must also be extended to Adam Marischuk, who spent many an hour editing and offering wise advice. Any errors or lapses are mine alone and can only be put down to not having heeded his advice or academic direction.

CONTENTS

सत्यमेव जयते

'Satyameva Jayate'

'Truth alone triumphs'

(National motto of India)

INDIAN NUMBER SYSTEM

A **crore** (abbreviated cr) = 10,000,000

A **lakh** = 100,000 and in India is written thus: 1,00,000

Large amounts of money are often written in terms of *crores*. For example, 150,000,000 is written as 'fifteen *crore* rupees', '15crore' or 'Rs 15 crore'

An <u>anna</u> was a currency unit formerly used in British India, equal to $\frac{1}{16}$ of a rupee. It was demonetised as a currency unit when India decimalised its currency in 1957.

Other coins were:

1 pice = $\frac{1}{4}$ anna = $\frac{1}{64}$ rupee.

1 anna = $\frac{1}{16}$ rupee.

15 rupees (approximately) = 1 mohur.

'It is in the nature of imperialism that citizens of the imperial power are always among the last to know – or care – about circumstances in the colonies.'

Bertrand Russell
Welsh philosopher
(1872-1970)

INTRODUCTION

Having now gauged the motives of British Empire in India in the previous two books in this series, from its commercial beginnings through its military phase of conquest and ultimately to its administrative end game, we are well placed to enter into debate concerning the successes and failures of the British Raj.

We have clearly ascertained that empire is not on the school curriculum in Britain, and so discussions surrounding the mores of its empire are rarely held because there are few people, beyond academic circles where the subject is well researched, that are properly versed in its history.

This essay on the audit of British India intends to expand horizons and serve as a platform from which improved understanding and further debate may spring. One of the primary objectives of education is for the student to answer their questions so they may go on to formulate more meaningful questions, and so it is with this brief foray into the many aspects of Indian life affected by British rule.

An almost classic summing up, in an absence of a wider public understanding of the issues involved in Britain's rule over India, often concludes with the final phrase, *"On balance, the British empire was a net good."*

One may well have already come to a firm opinion as to which side of the scales of justice to come down on after reading the previous two books in this series. The British government, moving forward, has made noises toward finally integrating Empire into the school curriculum. The call by many historians has been for it to be a 'balanced' approach, so that all aspects are touched upon, including the positive, despite certain ideologies that may find such mentions abhorrent.

Of course, in a classroom there should be no room for one-sided debates as the role of education is not just the rote learning of facts but the more important duty of promoting creative thinking. And by pitting contrasting viewpoints against one another, one can better arrive at the truth of a matter. It would seem obvious and unnecessary to state this, but such philosophy is presently under attack in the West. This was much was understood by Akbar the Great, the third Mughal ruler, who applied this principle through his famous religious debating chamber, Ibadat Khana. All main religious beliefs, including atheism, were encouraged to meet and present their arguments. The result for Akbar was that the wise ruler concluded that there is no absolute truth. Could this be the same for empire?

Everyone in India knows that the British ruled for 200 years. It was 190 years to be more precise, but certain numbers have symbolic and political significance. The dates taken for this calculation are Clive's victory at the battle of Plassey in 1757 up until the exit of the Crown from India in 1947. And yet this is not true either, but again it depends on your viewpoint.

Under the East India Company, Clive took control of Bengal, the rest of India laid far beyond their reach at that point. It would take a further one hundred years to conquer the rest of the sub-continent, finally defeating the Sikhs in 1849. But India was still, officially at least, in the hands of the East India Company.

Even by the time the British left, there was still two-fifths of the land under Princely rule, albeit indirectly controlled by the

British, so one could go to a stretch and say the British never ruled all of India, but the imperialists would disagree strongly at such blasphemy.

It wasn't until the advent of the 'Mutiny' in 1857, that the British government stepped in and rested control of India from The Company. With that in mind, one has to recalculate the duration of Great Britain's rule, and not Company control, over 'all' India and the figure is more than halved to a modest 90 years.

What comes as a surprise, perhaps, is that neither the native nationalists nor the British imperialists are happy with that outcome. This is because numbers possess an intrinsic influence over the human imagination. For the imperialist it is clear that almost halving the reach of British rule diminishes the prestige often associated, rightly or wrongly, with the ability of one group to take over another. Out of pride then Britain will not question the popular 200-year legacy. But neither will the nationalists touch the convenient, well-rounded number as it appeals to a greater sense of injustice and a louder rallying cry for modern nationalism. The greater the indignation, the more irresistible the pull of nationalism.

Just by looking at a simple fact of how long the British ruled in India, which should be little more than a simple calculation, has opened a can of worms of conflicting impressions, political exigencies and personal preferences. This small example, therefore, illustrates that the subject of empire and in this case, Britain's Indian empire, is nuanced. While there may well be areas that are black and white in their interpretations there are many others that are grey, and require time to consider their myriad possibilities. And on this last point there are many in Britain, as well as India, that agree.

CHAPTER

- I -

LOOT

"And the more I read the more I was filled with astonishment and indignation at the apparently conscious and deliberate bleeding of India by England throughout a hundred and fifty years. I began to feel that I had come upon the greatest crime in all history."[1]

In 2015 the Oxford Union put forward the motion *"This house believes Britain owes reparations to her former colonies."* The Indian writer, former UN diplomat and National Congress MP, Shashi Tharoor was invited to join the group to second the motion. His brief 15-minute speech went viral on YouTube, especially in his native India, when he succinctly destroyed the proposition that the Raj had been a benevolent rule that had benefitted India. For those brought up on wistful notions of Empire and rarely, if ever, exposed to divergent opinions on such matters the rapid-fire delivery of the mile-long list of wrong doing delivered by Tharoor, would have come as a nasty awakening. And all that despite the author's erudite and conciliatory tone.

Of course, polar opinions of 'all' bad and 'all' good are not helpful, nor rarely accurate. So, what was Mr. Tharoor missing from his extensive list?

The evidence over whether the British looted India, even amongst contemporary British sources, is extensive and self-inflicting. But were the British the worse foreign invaders in this respect? This is the question, and it needs answering, as it is an

---

[1] DURANT, Will, *A Case for India*, p. x

1

accusation often levelled against the British, singling them out for particular condemnation.

So, what of the looting before the British had arrived? Some writers give the impression this was a singularly British contribution to Indian history and that previous invaders must be judged differently because they stayed and spent their 'loot' in India. One can take serious issue with this.

"Having emerged from editing a four-volume encyclopaedia of all empires in human history, I can say categorically that no empires have pursued tender or altruistic policies."[1]

As Professor John Mackenzie states above, that puts the British on level pegging with other empires.

India, though, was not just invaded by the British nor was she looted solely by them either. Very often the cut off point in history is telling. Where a critique of the British Raj is concerned one often feels as if no wrong-doing occurred before the British arrived. This is cherry picking history.

Loot is a Hindu and Sanskrit word, which must infer that the Hindus looted in previous times. So this makes Robert Clive, the first Governor of the Bengal Presidency and the man who established the military and political supremacy of the East India Company (EIC), very much a *goonda* in the Bengali mode, and not a unique aberration. But who else swooped down from the Hindu Kush and looted the land before the British came in and did the same?

---

[1] MACKENZIE, John, *'Viewpoint: Why Britain does not owe reparations to India'*, BBC News website, (28 July, 2015)

In 985, Rajaraja I was crowned king of the Cholas, a southern empire based around Tanjore. They embarked upon the invasion of Sri Lanka and sacked its Buddhist capital of Anuradhapura, plundering its stupas. Then they moved northwards and involved themselves in the rivalries between the Western and Eastern Chalukyas. They left behind them a reputation for brutality, rapine and the massacring of women and children.

When Rajaraja's son, Rajendra I, succeeded him he invaded Sri Lanka anew and repeated his father's act of removing all the treasure of Lanka that they could find, nothing was deemed too sacred.

Then the Chola army pushed further north in order to retrieve the sacred water of the Ganga so that it could be used to bless Chola lands in the south. While there, they defeated the Buddhist Pala dynasty just west of Bengal and took more treasure and women, only to return south from whence they had come.

In the eighth century there were the Arab conquests of the Sind and raids into Gujarat and Rajasthan, but the major confrontations between Hindu and Islamic invaders would occur after the tenth century.

Then came Mahmud of Ghazni from Afghanistan. The name is well-known in India's history and arguably likened to the devil. The Ghaznavid Muslims, under Mahmud's father Sabuktigin, had raided the Shahi city of Lugham towards the close of the tenth century and did their religious duty to root out idolaters, by butchering the townspeople, torching the temples and looting the shrines. The plunder was so great they said that the fingers of those that counted it went numb from the cold.

Mahmud would carry out at least sixteen bloody raids into northern India, according to the historian and Secretary to Mahmud, Al-Utbi, to *'exalt the standard of religion, widen the plain of right, illuminate the words of truth, and strengthen the power of justice.'* In reality, they were to extend his control and provide finances for his army and fund his growing capital of Ghazni.

His greatest raid was in 1008 when he engulfed the Punjab and took the temple-city of Kangra, carrying away 180 kilos of gold ingots and two tonnes of silver bullion and coinage to the value of seventy million dirhams. Four years later Mahmud took Thanesar, north of Delhi, returning with treasure considered *'impossible to recount.'*

Six years on and Mahmud arrived in Mathura, a place of pilgrimage sacred to Lord Krishna. Mahmud ransacked its immense temple bedecked with riches. Once the temple had been picked clean of its wealth it was burned and razed to the ground, despite Mahmud declaring that it would have taken centuries and a fortune to have built such a grandiose structure. Then the later Sultan of Delhi, Sikinder Lodi, attacked Mathura, destroying the notorious white Temple built to honour Vishnu.

Mahmud moved on to the Ganga and sacked Kanuaj, returning home with twenty million dirhams, 53,000 slaves and 350 elephants.

Then came his most ambitious venture in 1024, when he entered deep into Gujarat and crossed the desert to take the temple site of Somnath by surprise. The slaughter was such that even Muslim chroniclers noted its severity. The booty amounted to two million dirhams in precious metals and gem stones; some say ten times that amount. Somnath was a place of pilgrimage and at its centre was its venerated *lingam*, the phallic sculpture representing Shiva. Mahmud then took it upon himself to smash the *lingam* and used the shattered pieces in the steps of the Jami Masjid mosque at Ghazni, evidently so that the faithful could trample it under foot when going to prayer. The British never carried out any sacrilege quite like this.

In fact, the British tried to restore the old gates taken from the temple by Mahmud. It was even debated in the House of Commons: *the Proclamation of the Gates*, as it was referred to in 1843. Edward Law, 1st Earl of Ellenborough, ordered the British army in Afghanistan to return via Ghazni and uproot the sandalwood gates to Somnath. On their triumphal arrival back in the Somnath temple the gates were judged to be replicas and not even of sandalwood. They now rest in a store-room in Agra Fort, calmly collecting dust.

One must now be thinking that if the British could attempt a magnanimous gesture such as this, then surely in the 21st century the modern democracy could do the same thing with similar items they had removed under comparable auspices of plunder that now rest in the British Museum.

In 1299, the Somnath temple was again sacked, this time by Al-ud-din Khilji and according to Tal-ul-Ma'sir of Hasan Nizami, the Sultan boasted that *'fifty-thousand infidels were dispatched to hell by the sword'* and *'more than twenty-thousand slaves, and cattle beyond all calculation fell into the hands of the victors.'*

In 1395, the temple was destroyed for a third time by Zafar Khan, the governor of Gujarat under the Delhi Sultanate. Once more it was rebuilt only for the Sultan of Gujarat, Mahmud Begada, in 1451 to desecrate it.

Finally, the Somnath temple was one of many destined for destruction by Emperor Aurangzeb's dictum in 1665. Then he issued another order in 1702, stating that should Hindu worship renew there, then what was left of the temple would be completely removed.

In 1030, the iconoclastic Mahmud passed away, much to the relief, no doubt, of the many temple keepers across the north-western frontier of India.

Next to make an impression upon the fearful record of Indian history was Muhammad of Ghor, of Turkic extraction. He was as much the iconoclast as Mahmud and equally responsible for the further abolition of temple complexes in India.

When Muhammad of Ghor defeated the kingdom of Prithviraj in the 12th century the rest of the Punjab and northern India laid open. There were scenes of massacre and pillage and within a year Delhi had been taken. Muhammad's Turkish general built the Qubbat-ul-Islam (Dome of Islam) mosque to commemorate the Afghan victory over the Rajputs and had, as a Persian inscriptions says, 27 Hindu and Jain temples removed and their pieces incorporated into the new structure. It was the first mosque built in Delhi.

The Ghorids also went on to sack the Gujarati capital of Anhilwara. At Varanasi, according to the chronicler Ferishta, the Ghorid army destroyed all the temples' idols, rededicating the shrines to the *'one true God'*. However, no sooner had they conquered these territories than they receded back to their capital, carrying off fourteen-hundred camel loads of treasure.

In 1194, Mohammad of Ghor's general, Qutb-ud-din Aibak, demolished the Vishwanath temple, which was one of the twelve *Jyotirlingas*, the holiest of Shiva temples. It was rebuilt but again destroyed this time in the 15th century. It was rebuilt once more during the reign of Akbar the Great but his great-grandson, the sixth Mughal ruler, Aurangzeb destroyed it definitively in 1669 and built the Gyanvapi mosque on the site.

That, however, is not the end of the story, despite Aurangzeb's mosque still being in place today. The temple was rebuilt yet again in 1780 on an adjacent site by Ahilyabai Holkar, the Holkar Queen of the land-locked Maratha Malwa kingdom in the north. Her father-in-law, Malhar Rao Holkar, a noble of the Maratha empire, had planned to demolish the mosque and rebuild the temple on the original site.

At the turn of the 13th century the Khaljis had also arrived in northern India from Afghanistan, tribal rivals of the Ghorids, and struck into Bihar and Bengal. One conquest saw them massacre the inhabitants of the famous Buddhist monastery complex of Odantapuri and relieve it of all its treasure in the process. They captured Nadia, the capital of the Senas and their other city of importance, Lakhnauti. In 1296, under Ala-ud-din, they sacked and plundered the city of Devagiri where king Rama-chandra kept the fortune of the Seunas.

They besieged and overcame the Rajput fortresses of Chitor, Jalor and Ranthambhor and even turned the tide on the invading Mongols, which in India were known as Mughals.

In 1298, they overcame the Gujarat and duly emptied it of its riches. Eleven years later, led by Malik Kafur, they attacked the Kakatiyas of Andhra, famous for its diamond mines. And after routing its army, they left with hoards of treasure. Kafur then turned his attentions on the Hoysalas, who preferred negotiations and after paying tribute joined forces as Kafur headed south into Tamil Nadu. Despite being unable to engage the Pandyan king in battle, Kafur's forces did manage to strip the temples of Chidambaram, Madurai and Srirangam of their golden idols. When Kafur arrived back in Delhi the spoils were estimated to be 214 tonnes of gold, twenty-thousand horse, 612 elephants, and innumerable caskets of jewellery.

Muhammad bin Tughluq, the Sultan of Delhi from 1325 to 1351, was also known as 'Muhammad the Bloody' and one of India's more controversial Muslim rulers due to his wild policy swings. Ibn Batuta, the famous jurist and traveller, the Arab world's Marco Polo from Morocco, was appointed Chief Justice of Delhi by Muhammad and praised the ruler's liberality, despite fearing for his life at one point.

Muhammad's religious tolerance has also been called into question and he has both detractors and defendants. The tyrant, intellectual, benefactor, whatever you will, was succeeded by his cousin Feroz Shah, who would sack the great shrine of Lord Jagannath at Puri and carry out massacres among the local population. But Feroz Shah also innovated and developed his territory ensuring an increase in the welfare of his people.

In the ensuing chaos following the death of Feroz the land was eventually invaded in 1398 by a Mongol army under Timur the Lame and the city of Delhi was given over to scenes of murder and rapine. During the three-day depravity, the Muslim areas were spared while the Hindu quarters were either put to the sword or enslaved.

In 1473, the Gujarat Sultan, Mahmud Begada, took the city of Dwarka and proceeded to destroy its temple. Here the British looted the temple in 1859 when they ousted the Vaghers, but two years later they would actually reverse their irreverent act by refurbishing the *shikhara*, which was the rising tower typical in northern Hindu temples and where the presiding deity is enshrined.

Then came Babur, the fifth-generation descendant of Timur on his father's side and a distant relative of Genghis Khan on his mother's. He came into the Punjab in 1505 from his Afghan stronghold and ultimately secured the Mughal dynasty in India.

The name of Babur was revived in the international press in 1992 when his mosque, Ayodhya, was destroyed by a Hindu mob on the shaky grounds that it occupied the very place where Lord Rama had been born.

Even the impressive Akbar the Great succumbed to giving free reign to massacre at the siege of Chitor in 1567-8, where some 20,000 civilians were rumoured to have been slaughtered.

Akbar, the third Mughal emperor, reigned from 1556 to 1605. He is one of the bright lights of enlightened rule and rightly deserves his epithet of 'the Great' through his conciliatory policies to unite his vast empire. He was learned and his three courts were awash with culture and intellectuals. He became disillusioned with Islam as he aged and sought another spiritual route by creating the syncretic religion of the *Din-i Ilahi*, meaning Religion of God or Divine Faith, in 1582. It merged of elements from the religions of his empire, primarily Islam and Hinduism, but also elements from Christianity, Jainism and Zoroastrianism, which asserted an underlying unity and sought to reconcile the differences that divided his subjects.

The Mughal family, however, was not a happy one. Jahangir, Akbar's son, tried to seize power while Akbar was still on the throne. Later, following his father's death, Jahangir pursued his eldest son, Prince Khusrau, who had in turn, tried to oppose him (a case of like father, like son) and had his eyes put out.

When Jahangir's son Shah Jahan, of Taj Mahal fame, came to the throne he had his one remaining brother and all male cousins put to death. It would come as no surprise then, that in later years all four of his sons moved against him and the victor, Aurangzeb, not only killed his squabbling siblings but also imprisoned his father in Agra's Red Fort. With family like that, who needed the British?

In fact, the Mughals followed a long-established pattern in northern India, for the majority of conflicts were not so much foreign invaders seeking plunder, but rather outbreaks of internecine strife. It was not the *Pax Mughala* some would like us to believe, and certainly not comparable to the security eventually brought by the British to internal Indian affairs.

Aurangzeb would be the last of the conquering Mughals and with him India saw a decline in its temple destruction and desecration. He did not possess the worldly wisdom of Akbar and has largely been remembered for his solipsistic religious zeal. He undid much of the good done by his great-grandfather, while doing much to drive a wedge between Muslim and Hindu populations even before the British were accused of being the sole font of such religious discontent.

Hindus clearly came under attack. Aurangzeb replaced Hindus with Muslims in the local administrations, penalised Hindu merchants through more stringent taxes than the Muslims were subjected to, reimposed the tax on Hindu pilgrims, which Akbar had done away with, cancelled the endowments made to temples and Brahmins, and reinstated the *jizya* tax levied on all non-Muslims.

Most notoriously of all, though, temples were torn down. The most famous shrine that was replaced by a mosque was that of Vishvanatha in Varanasi, a town considered the *'Athens of India'* according to François Bernier, the personal physician to Mughal prince Dara Shikoh, due to its relevance as the centre of Hindu teaching. In the city of Mathura another Aurangzeb mosque occupies the site where once the Keshava Deo temple stood. Despite having been rebuilt under the reign of Akbar and destroyed by Aurangzeb, Mathura would be restored to its former glory under the British Raj.

Further temples were ordered removed and mosques erected in their places at Ellora, Trimbakeshwar, Narasinghpur and Pandaharpur.

Other notable losses were the Sitaramji temple at Soron in Uttar Pradesh, the shrine of Devi Patan at Gonda, the Chausath Yogini temple and its now headless idols. The Harshnath temple was also destroyed in 1679 and the intricate Someshwar temple in Rajasthan was pulled down a year later.

The temple complex of Hampi, now a UNESCO World Heritage Site, situated within the ruins of the city of Vijayanagara, the former capital of the Vijayanagaran empire, is the most symbolic monument of Karnataka. Its ornate gateways, palaces and temples now lie in ruins since it was attacked by the Deccan sultanates in 1565. The city was captured, its temples plundered and an estimated 100,000 Hindus massacred. The Vijayanagaran empire did, however, continue to exist but suffered a slow decline and the temple city was never rebuilt or returned to.

'Akbar [had] disrupted the Muslim community by recognising that India was not an Islamic country: Aurangzeb disrupted India by behaving as if it were.'[2]

The British may have favoured the *Mohammedan* over the *Hindoo* for purposes of securing support for their rule and a distraction for the populace, but there was no interfering in either's religious practices. The Company had always resisted doing this and despite the Crown allowing Christian

---

[2] GASCOIGNE, B., *The Great Moghuls*, p.127

missionaries into the country and the fears of the natives that the British were up to something, there was no direct attack on either of India's main religions.

The several centuries of Muslim rule in India do not follow a uniform pattern and subsequently defy any attempt at oversimplification. During the 14th century rule of Muhammad bin Tughlug there was oppression. Idolatry may have been reviled but Hinduism was not banned. There was the *jizya* tax levied on non-Muslims, but it was not uniformly applied in each Muslim area or by the various Islamic rulers. Further, the effect of Muslim rule on the Hindu in terms of religion, culture, tolerance and violence are controversial issues to this day. Therefore, there is no easy answer.

Above all, there is no issue more contentious than that of temple desecration and destruction at the hands of the Muslims. The historian Richard Eaton knows what a conflict-ridden topic this is. The commonly held belief is that the Muslims indiscriminately razed thousands of temples to the ground. Eaton has found concrete evidence of just 80, from 1192 onwards. Then there comes the reasoning behind it. Was it religious zeal or political expediency? Temples were bank vaults for rulers as well as vestiges of power. Some medieval historians make a clear link between recent conquest and temples being destroyed. That is to say, the temples were only destroyed as a means to undermine the previous ruler or as a punishment if he had defied his overlord. And there are many such examples. However, Aurangzeb's measures sometimes, but not always, contradict that generalised view.

The British may have picked Delhi's Red Fort clean during the 1857 siege and looted the city of Jhansi the following year, but temple desecration and destruction was not a British act. So when making comparisons between the British and those that came before, on this score, there can be no outright condemnation of the British.

Of Indian loot, the Victoria and Albert Museum in London holds the largest collection (over 40,000 items) of Indian art treasures outside the subcontinent. Most provided by the defunct India Museum. Other elements are to be found in the British Museum, such as the ancient sculptures from the stupa at Amaravati. They are one of the *'earliest and greatest masterpieces of Buddhist art'* and date from the first to third centuries AD. To this the British had even planned to add no less than pieces of the Taj Mahal itself, that *'tear on the face of eternity'* as Tagore described it. Thankfully, this last abomination did not go ahead, due to lack of commercial interest.

BALANCING THE BOOKS

At the forefront of the Nationalist argument against British rule in India has been the fact that India's GDP took a nose-dive after the British arrived on the sub-continent. In 1600, the year of the inception of the EIC, India's share of world GDP stood at 22.4% as listed in the now-famous study of world GDP, spanning from 1AD to 2008 by the British economist Angus Maddison. From 1500 to 1600 India's GDP had grown by 22.7% and the following century saw a 22.2% growth. And then from 1700 to 1800 it registered 21%. The growth rate was stable even with the EIC expanding its territorial control over India. Things, however, would soon change. And for diverse reasons.

The first thing of note is that it makes perfect sense for both India and China to possess the largest share of world GDP due to their significant populations. When production levels depended on the number of hands available for work, the largest populations would, naturally, come out on top. But then the Industrial Revolution entered to level the playing field.

Steam power would tip the balance in favour of Europe. It was, after all, the greatest revolution in human history since the advent of agriculture, and it freed man from the toil and sweat of tilling the land. In 1881, the German statistician Dr. Ernst Engels computed *from the best and fullest materials at his command* that there existed horsepower equivalent to that of 47 billion labouring men. That implied that the effort of one worker with such steam power could now achieve the results of

117 workers, and the stats were compiled in such a way as to *'err on the side of defect rather than exaggeration'*.

Now, if we consider that the Lion's share of that steam power was concentrated in Europe and the greater share of that power was in Britain, are we seriously saying that such a multiplication in force and productive energy holds no bearing over the world GDP swinging from East to West, or are we to believe that it is little more than colonial intervention stunting Asian growth?

The USA has the lead on technology and has implemented it to great effect, outcompeting European rivals with it, but there has never been a territorial occupation holding Europe back. Therefore, how could 300,000,000 Indians compete with the Industrial Revolution? Asia's GDP was, therefore, bound to fall.

'With such vast reservoirs of productive capacity to draw upon, the human race has no right to cherish Malthusian fears, for this reservoir is only one of the many others created by the inventive powers of the mind and is as yet imperfectly utilized.'[1]

It was a foregone conclusion that the balance of world GDP would now move West until the East caught up in technological terms. Britain ensured, however, in the case of India that this would be a long time off in the future by deliberately hindering those industries that offered most competition to hers, but not all. India had been the world's leading exporter of textiles and Britain would turn her into a dependent importer of cheaply machined alternatives. The effect was double. Firstly, there was Britain's incomparable advantage created by steam power and then the capping of India's industry to ensure a captive market.

---

[1] WELLING, James C., 'The Law of Malthus', *American Anthropologist*, Vol. 1, No. 1 (Jan., 1888) p.20

Nevertheless, India's GDP share of the world market would have slowed despite British meddling.[2]

Then there comes the conflictive point about the true nature of India's wealth. It is maintained that India was a rich 'country', and there was evident wealth widely remarked upon by travellers, from the Moroccan Ibn Batuta in his famous *The Travels,* to the Europeans, but what about the average Indian? Was the land labourer *ryot* living the life of Riley, as some would have us believe with precious stones being peddled on the streets as if they were vegetables? The lack of precedent for such a thing in all human history is significant here.

'In 1AD, India's GDP per capita was $450, as was China's. But Italy under the Roman Empire had a per capita income of $809. In 1000AD, India's per capita income was $450 and China's was $466. But the average West Asian countries, such as Turkey and Iraq, were much higher at $621. In terms of general prosperity, therefore, it was the Arab world that was doing well a millennium ago. The Caliphate of Baghdad was a centre of power at the time and both science and culture flourished.'[3]

Per capita income is a much surer test of a Nation's prosperity; one would always prefer to be on average wages in the UAE than the USA.

Renaissance Italy, come the 16th century, saw a rise to $1,100 in per capita income. But then came the dawn of the 17th century with first the Dutch, then the British attaining hegemony in word trade. The Netherlands saw a per capita

---

[2] 'According to historical GDP estimates by economist Angus Maddison, India's GDP during the British Raj grew in absolute terms but declined in relative share to the world. From 1850 to 1947 India's GDP per capita had **grown** only slightly by 16%, from $533 to $618 in 1990 international dollars.' (*Economy of India under the British Raj*, Wikipedia)
[3] CHAKRAVARTY, Manas, *The Hindustan Times-LiveMint*, Aug. 25, 2010

income in 1600 of $1,381 and England of $984. From this increase we can see that Europe is now on the rise and this is before any colonial surplus is feeding into their economies. Europe is now the centre of ideas, technology and science.

But what was India's per capita income? One would infer from Nationalist discourse that it was the highest in the world and was about to be smashed by the incoming British, and yet it still sat at $550, where it had remained stagnant for centuries. This was the same picture for China at $600 in the year 1600. Their previous share of world GDP, as suspected, was purely due to demographics and Western technological advances were encroaching ever more on that age-old allocation of manpower.

The British did eventually have a negative effect on what share was left of India's global GDP through mercantilist tactics such as removing protectionist import tariffs, but the sub-continent's decline was already well underway before any Englishman set foot on the sub-continent.

'Using Tharoor's logic, the US should be affronted that its share of global economic output has fallen from almost 33% in 1945 to about 15% now. And when it comes to the decline of manufacturing, well, few countries know better than Britain in the modern era what happens when you are outcompeted by foreign rivals who produce more cheaply than you.'[4]

But of course, even to say that India up until the advent of the British had the greatest cut of world GDP is to distort the data. Firstly, India didn't even exist as a political entity and then to pit it against the GDP of individual states in Europe is to misrepresent it still further. It is a more balanced argument to

---

[4] Comment on review of Tharoor's *Inglorious Empire* from internet user

compare the 'area' of India with that of Europe down through the ages and here we find the pie is evenly split between India, Europe and China.

By 1947, though, Britain's GDP was three times that of India's and that dramatic change cannot be explained away by technological dominance alone.

By 2008, India's GDP per capita, according to Maddison's estimates, stood at $2,975, a little above a third of the world average. This shows that India was getting back on her feet and one could say was faring better under her own steam, which is not only what one would expect to see but would also hope to hear. This increase, though, has only come about due to a reversal of Indian economic policy, ditching Nehruvian socialism and embracing globalisation. In doing so, India espoused the liberal policies the British had pioneered a century earlier, thus making India one of the beneficiaries of, what historian Niall Ferguson terms, 'anglobalisation'.

'And on the other side of the balance sheet were the immense British investments in Indian infrastructure, irrigation and industry. By the 1880s the British had invested £270 million in India, not much less than one-fifth of their entire investments overseas. By 1914 the figure had reached £400 million.'[5]

But as India was a captive market, one could see this as little more than a racket with India paying excessive rates for such 'investment'. At one time India had had a vibrant financial sector with a network of agents, brokers and middlemen, until the Raj had dismantled it. This sector would have no doubt involved itself extensively in such development, but it was

---

[5] FERGUSON, Niall, *Empire: How Britain Made the Modern World*, (Penguin, 2003) p.216

nowhere to be seen. The City of London, naturally and willingly, filled the void.

'True, the average Indian had not got much richer under British rule. Between 1757 and 1947 British per capita gross domestic product had increased 347 per cent, Indian by a mere 14 per cent.'[6]

Much has been said of the notorious 'Drain' of surplus profit back to Britain in the form of Home Charges, and that this is something that cannot be levelled at India's Muslim rulers as they spent their money in the country. However, the British did leave India an impressive infrastructure and its efficient Civil Service, which can now be weighed against the bureaucracy of a modern, free India. And one must ask the question: is there any corruption in Indian politics today?

TATA motors, the largest automobile manufacturer in India, today no doubt remits its Jaguar–Land Rover profits back to India as does Rites, a subsidiary of the Indian railways, who offer their technological expertise to Rendel, the principal technology consultant for Britain's railways. But this reallocation of money abroad is called profit, not 'tribute' or 'drain'.

'To treat these remittances as an economic loss is to apply a law to India which is accepted in no other country in the world. The profits of the business are the property of the owner to do with as he pleases, and it is has never occurred to any human being that the foreign investor who derives profit from American cattle ranches or South-African gold-mines is thereby robbing the United States or the Transvaal.'[7]

---

[6] Ibid., p.217
[7] CURZON, Lord, *The North American Review*, Vol. 192, No. 657 (Aug.,1910) p.160

It has been argued by traditional historians that the payments made to Britain by India were in lieu of military and civilian services and capital investments. However, we have seen how a captive market does not find the most competitive price once it is sheltered from the free forces of capitalism. The Civil Servants were also handsomely rewarded far beyond their European counterparts for work, not entirely executed with the greatest propensity.

It is furthermore believed that had India maintained its own army and navy, it would have cost more, but no figures are offered to back up this simple knee-jerk conjecture. The same argument is offered when comparing a president over a monarch.

Britain did, however, use India's trade surplus to finance its trade deficit with the rest of the world, and this point cannot be easily overlooked. It was this surplus, the agricultural surplus, that had it stayed in the country would have ensured the next step towards its own industrial revolution as the towns would have been able to sustain greater numbers. A food surplus is needed to maintain an urban population, who will work the mills and machines essential for modern industrial output. This never happened in India because the British purchased that precious surplus for their own purposes. There does not seem to be any controversy covering this point either, and it is a damning piece of evidence. But again, by way of a brief disclaimer, it is upheld that this surplus was compensated for by the import of gold and silver that went into private Indian hands. Therefore India was remunerated.

CHAPTER

- III -

UNDER CONSTRUCTION

The British laid the railways (more than any other colonial power in their territories) constructed canals, the Lahore to Calcutta highway, not to mention the many bridges which illustrated Franklin Roosevelt's quote that, *"There can be little doubt that in many ways the story of bridge building is the story of civilisation. By it, we can readily measure a people's progress."*

Of special note are the Duffering bridge, the Howrah bridge, the Sutlej bridge (now in Pakistan) and the Victoria bridge amongst many others. Yes, of course, these could easily have been built by India herself, but the point here is that they are all examples of internal investment of Indian money. Initially, it was British capital that met the costs but that capital was eventually repaid from Indian revenues, so one can never make the claim, as is often the case, that British investors built India when it was the ordinary Indian that repaid that investment at what were abnormally higher rates of interest. But, nonetheless, the money *was* spent in India, just as the Mughals had spent their revenues.

"...the capital which the British merchant has supplied to India is a net gain to the country in the resources developed, the consumption created, the labour employed and the wages paid."[1]

---

[1] Ibid., p.160

To be fair we have seen that canal building (even though India had the largest system in the world by 1914) should have been greater, as with road building, so there is no room for complacency here, but the projects were undertaken for the eventual benefit of India. It is tangible worth of India's revenue taken from her by her British overlords and then returned as value added to her GNP.

'for every rupee remitted India has received a full and fair equivalent in goods, services or capital'[1]

There can also be cause for celebrating the irrigation carried out in the Punjab under British rule. The Government of India harnessed the area's five rivers, which is what the name Punjab means, and transformed six million acres of desert into one of the richest agricultural tracts in all Asia.

'The British increased the area of irrigated land by a factor of eight, so that by the end of the Raj a quarter of all land was irrigated, compared with just 5 per cent of it under the Mughals.'[2]

This, however, can only be celebrated in part. While it did advance agriculture, it more importantly diverted the economy away from possible industrial development, which could have benefitted the regional economy to a greater extent.

That said, by 1914 India had the third largest railway system in the world, the world's largest jute manufacturing system in

---

[1] BROOKS, Sydney, 'American Opinion and British Rule in India', *The North American Review*, Vol. 190, No. 649 (Dec., 1909) p.777
[2] FERGUSON, Niall, p.216

the world, the fourth largest cotton textile industry and 2.5% of world trade.[3]

There were evident advances in India due to British intervention. Admittedly, numerous of these were merely the side effects of the need for deepening military control and organizational efficiency for better exploitation.

'The British, by contrast, brought tangible development, ports and railways, which created the basis for a modern state. More important, they brought the framework for parliamentary democracy that Indians, who already possessed indigenous traditions of heterodoxy and pluralism, were able to fit to their own needs. Indeed, the very Hindu pantheon, with its many gods rather than one, works toward the realization that competing truths are what enable freedom. Thus, the British, despite all their flaws, advanced an ideal of Indian greatness.'[4]

The railways, however, should have been taken to India and not forced them upon the people. The rest of the world managed to lay their own track without the need for invasion. It only stands to reason that India would also have covered her landscape with railways; perhaps later rather than sooner, but that does not excuse the British policy of making the Indian taxpayer contribute to something that had been provided elsewhere by the private investor. Had the British done that and gone down a transparent capitalist route by affording the railways at the cheapest price to India, then such an

---

[3] DAS, Gurcharan, Essay - *India: How a rich nation became poor and will be rich again* (March 19, 2007) Author of *India Unbound* (Knopf, New York, 2001)
[4] KAPLAN, Robert D., *India's New Face* – The Atlantic (April 2009)

achievement would have been one of the glories of Britain's industrial age.

'It may be argued very plausibly that some institutions that came under British rule, such as the railways, would have come even without such rule. After all, many modern institutions fell into place in Iran, nineteenth-century Latin America, China, Japan or parts of South East Asia (e.g. Thailand) that were not colonised. Why is it a plausible assumption then that Britons, whose primary allegiance was to Britain, would have done better for India than Indians? Would any historian of Britain be willing to accept, say, that Britain would have performed better economically if only she were ruled over by Indians?'[5]

It is argued that India would have had the railways anyway, which is true. You only have to take the case of Thailand that was never colonised by the Europeans, and neither was France and both countries have rail lines. However, would India have possessed as much track and laid it in such a short time period? Again, it is almost irrelevant because the British built the railways initially to transport the military and then to serve their economy and freight. It was not developed for the carrying of passengers. The British Government of India, in fact, penalised passenger lines through different tariffs. They were simply not interested in it and yet it is the carrying of peoples for which the lines are synonymous today. If anything, it looks as if the British didn't build enough.

In conclusion, though, the most relevant point is that the British undertook immense railway construction, leaving a net gain to India. It is yet another example of the British spending

---

[5] SUBRAHMANYAM, Sanjay, 'Empires Good And Evil', *The Times of India* (Jul 21, 2005)

India's money in India. Had they not done that then they would have left India in a worse state than they did in 1947.

Assam, the home of tea growing, had been a jungle in 1840 but by 1900 four million acres were under cultivation. And there were also great areas of north east India placed under irrigation due to British intervention, where some 500,000 acres of the Ganges plains were farmed for the Asian opium trade, a further black spot on the exploitative nature of the British Empire. The irrigation accomplishments have been termed by one historian as among the *'greatest monuments to British rule.'* But as we can see they too are not without their blemishes.

And so is blemished the Assam tea plantations today[6] with accusations of child labour, workers suffering from malnutrition, poor housing conditions, low pay and spraying chemicals without adequate protection. It seems modern India in this area fares little better than imperial Britain.

"Never," said Lord Curzon, "let us shut our eyes to the poverty and the misery of India. But do not let us be so blind to the truth as not to see that there is an enormous improvement, that there is everywhere more money in the country, in circulation, in reserves, in investments, in deposits and the pockets of the people; that the wages of labor have risen, that the standards of living among the poorest have gone up, that they employ conveniences and even luxuries which a quarter of a century ago were undreamed of, thereby indicating an all-round

---

[6] In 2015, a joint investigation by Radio 4's *File on Four* and *BBC News* in Assam, north-east India into workers' conditions in India's tea plantations, uncovered the conditions mentioned above. In January, 2014, Columbia Law School's Human Rights Institute published a major study into conditions on estates part-owned Tata. In April 2016, the Duke and Duchess of Cambridge on an official visit to India had planned on going to a tea plantation but were advised against the visit owing to the concern over workers' welfare.

increase of purchasing power and showing wherever taxation could be held to pinch we have reduced it, and may perhaps be able to do so still more. It is only fairness to acknowledge these facts; it is blind prejudice to ignore them."[7]

The main cities which the British built, in large part, from the ground up were Madras (1644), Bombay (1661) and Calcutta (1690). Again this is substantial net worth added to the nation state and if cities are the engines of growth and the surest way to defeat poverty, then the British, while not making strident gains in these areas, at least laid the basis for natives to build upon. In addition, the British added extensively to already pre-existing Indian infrastructure where they had an important presence, such as in New Delhi, Bangalore and Secunderabad, adjoining Hyderabad. There was also substantial development in the capitals of the many Princely states where the British built areas, known as Residencies, to garrison troops and headquarter administrations. India's two megacities today are Mumbai and Chennai, which clearly have their roots in British colonialism and mature links to global commerce, also initiated by Britain.

Curzon restored the Taj Mahal and Fatehpur Sikri and went on to erect the Victoria Memorial in Calcutta. The same Lord Curzon, who had come to make an impact on the ICS (Indian Civil Service) and left saying that British rule, *"may be good for us; but is neither equally, nor altogether, good for them."*

Herbert Baker and Edwin Lutyens built New Delhi and its crowning glory the Viceroy's (now President's) House, *'the British Empire's one architectural masterpiece'* according to Niall

---

[7] BROOKS, Sydney, 'American Opinion and British Rule in India', p.781

Ferguson. The new city complex cost millions and has been taken over by the new Indian government, so it is obviously something that pleases the eye as it hasn't been burnt down yet. It is also another addition to net value.

There were other contributions to infrastructure that were clear additions to the GNP and of practical use for the everyday Indian. The telegraph system: 100,000 lines carried 17 million messages a year by the early twentieth century. In India the telegram, known as a 'taar', was still used until 2013.

It is true that the British did away with certain trades for which India was renowned, such as ship building and textile manufacture, industries they put asunder through protective tariffs on incoming British goods, but some would have fallen behind technologically and succumbed to greater external competition. This is a natural process of economic development and has affected all economies and sectors of industry at some point. Not everything changes because an imperial power wills it.

So the British de-industrialised India, or did they? In order to de-industrialise something it must first be industrialised and this was not the case in India when the British arrived.

'Despite a dynamic and a growing commercial sector which responded to market forces and extensive foreign trade, the truth is that 18th century India was significantly behind Western European technology, institutions and ideas. Neither an agricultural revolution, nor a scientific revolution had occurred, and in the long-run the manual skill of the Indian artisan could be no substitute for technological progress.'[8]

---

[8] DAS, Gurcharan, Essay – *'India: How a rich nation became poor and will be rich again'* (March 19, 2007) Author of *India Unbound* (Knopf, New York, 2001)

Ships were built to an extraordinary quality, India possessed the world's best cotton yarn and in large quantities, but these were handicrafts, not to be confused with the mechanised industrial-scale production, which was the great economic revolution of the age and was bound to tip the balance in favour of those possessing such technology, not to mention those that had invented it, namely the British.

'European industrial production was unassailable worldwide because of the cheapness of the product. Craft production like handloom weaving was destroyed everywhere, including in Britain itself.'[9]

In the case of India, Britain merely hastened the decline and then, uniquely, ensured there would be no recovery. That said there were industries that the British began in India such as introducing the first mills for raw cotton and jute, which gave employment to a million people and a further half a million on the railways. In the case of jute, particularly, which had been a mainstay of Dundee industry, the factory owners shifted production to India, laying off local Dundee workers. There was no interventionalism on the part of the British government to halt or reverse the trend.

India's coal industry was also started by the British, mining 16 million tons a year by 1914. The British also brought coffee, sugar and introduced large-scale tea production to India. In the case of tea, under colonial rule, India became a greater producer than China. However, it was a free India in the 1950s that converted it to the national drink that it is today. A poor quality harvest in the 1950s meant it was unsuitable for export, forcing

---

[9] MACKENZIE, John, 'Viewpoint: Why Britain does not owe reparations to India', *BBC News website*, (28 July, 2015)

the Tea Board to think outside the tin. They decided to promote it for internal consumption and the Indians took to it at once. Today 70% of all Indian tea is produced for the home market.

It is often claimed that the British brought both opium and alcohol to India. The Portuguese in 1600 were the first to observe the wide use of opium in India and its importance, while the oldest alcoholic drink in India is Indian mead, dating back to 4,000 BCE.

In the case of opium, The East India Company established a monopoly on the trade and actually achieved a reduction of consumption in India, primarily, because they needed as much of the produced opium for sale in China, where it commanded a higher price and the profits returned would offset any balance of payments. In Burma the British offered it for free to create a demand. Gandhi vociferously opposed such trade and campaigned for the British to ban opium in India.

It was said that if the British departed from India, they would leave no monument of their stay but empty beer-bottles. This was supposed to refer to the idea that India had gained nothing from British colonialism. However, despite the difficult measures in India around selling alcohol, the natives enjoy their tipple as well. By volume, India is the world's ninth-largest consumer of alcohol, according to IWSR Drinks Market Analysis, a London-based research firm, and the nation is second largest consumer of spirits (whisky, vodka, gin, rum, tequila, liqueurs), behind China. In fact, India is the world's largest consumer of whisky, drinking three times as much as the second biggest consumer, and that is the United States.

A free press is often claimed as another benefit bestowed upon India through colonialism owing to the British tradition of free speech. In fact, once the machinery and culture of the newspaper had been installed it was soon used against the government. In 1860, there were the Sedition laws, which ended the 'dream' of India's free press. And then in 1919 came the Rowlatt Act, which again closed down free speech the moment. It was clear that the moment the press had become a reality that the Indian became a voracious consumer of such media and an adept practitioner of the journalistic craft, with at one time there being as many as 8,000 native journals rolling off the presses.

CHAPTER
- IV -

ROOTING OUT POVERTY

One would think that the list of failures on the part of the British had all been exhausted by now; if only that were true. And yet, one of the Empire's greatest controversies has not even been mentioned - until now. It is a bone of great contention if it were proved to be true and that is the origin of India's poverty.

'There is no easy answer to the problem that the country was prosperous and the people were poor. One explanation is that even in the 18th century India had a large population and plenty of cheap labour. Prosperity comes with rising productivity and a rise in productivity depends on technology.'[1]

Had one not read about British India and Britain's role in its administration and its famine policy, it would be easy to believe the theory of Malthusian economy and that the inordinate size of the population is to blame. However, it is hard to look elsewhere for any other cause than colonial rule.

'One-fifth of the human race suffering poverty and oppression billerer than any to be found elsewhere on the earth. I was horrified. I had not thought it possible that any government could allow its subjects to sink to such misery.'[2]

---

[1] DAS, Gurcharan, *India: How a rich nation became poor and will be rich again.* Essay (2007)
[2] DURANT, Will, p. ix

We have, however, already noted conflicting opinions between observers and academics on the state of India before and during British rule. Who is correct? Why is there such divergence? To answer such questions would require a separate book but they must be engaged here, albeit briefly, to give good account and leave no stone unturned. To not engage in this issue, perhaps *the* issue pertinent to modern India in the wake of Empire, would be to avoid one of the most important lessons.

'The poverty of the masses of the peoples of India is, it is true, abject and pitiable enough. But to charge it to British rule is grotesque. I have shown that under British rule prosperity is slowly but steadily advancing. I have shown that the sum paid into the treasury by the inhabitants of British India in rent and taxes combined is less than $1 a head per annum, and that of this sum the peasant, who represents three-fourths of the population, contributes on an average, I should judge, less than one-half. Taxation, therefore, cannot be the cause of Indian poverty.'[1]

Professor B.R. Tomlinson in his 1988 article *The Historical Roots of Indian Poverty*, after lamenting the fact that the number of Imperial history courses in the UK has dropped, sees that there are two basic questions that needed answering, namely why has *'the process of structural economic change in the rural economy over the last one hundred years been slow?'* and although there had been *'uneven economic growth... why have its long-run distributional effects apparently been so perverse?'* And to answer that last point it was necessary to first consider the extent to which the different social structures that had grown out of

---

[1] BROOKS, Sydney, 'American Opinion and British Rule in India', *The North American Review*, Vol. 190, No. 649 (Dec., 1909) p.782

colonialism, and its favouritism, explained India's poverty today.

Professor Tomlinson saw modern India's poverty growing out of events in the agrarian economy between the two world wars, especially the Tsunami effect of the Wall Street Crash. The Depression marked *'a clear break in the history of the political economy of Indian agriculture, as the liquidity crisis that accompanied the collapse of international prices disrupted the existing mechanisms of export-led primary production.'*[2]

This led to the increase of inefficient methods of share-cropping in the 1930s, which would have meant a subsequent decrease in agricultural production. Payment in cash also reverted to that of in kind. The price of cash crops fell while food grains rose. This left the rural poor vulnerable. On the one hand, the export market no longer provided an outlet for small-holders to obtain sufficient returns for their labour in order to procure food, rent etc. and on the other, they now entered into direct competition with the burgeoning urban populations and their increased demand for food-grains, which forced prices higher.

Professors Vakil and Brahmananda from the Bombay School postulated the Wage-goods model in 1976 to counteract the Nehru-Mahalanobis model, which focused on capital and heavy goods. The latter was put into practice following Independence under Nehru's government and was still active until the 1990s.

In its essence the professors called for greater investment in wage-goods, which are, in the main, every day consumables (especially agricultural produce) such as food grains, pulses, cereals, milk and milk products, edible oils, fish, eggs, meat,

---

[2] TOMLINSON, B.R., *The Historical Roots of Indian Poverty: Issues in the Economic and Social History of Modern South Asia: 1880–1960,* Cambridge University Press (November, 2008) pp.134-5

sugar, sugar products, fruits, vegetables, spices, tea, coffee, cloth, matches, soap, salt and even kerosene. This would provide effective employment for the many surplus hands in the economy and thereby afford a much-needed escape route out of poverty.

In their wage-goods model they stated that,

'Poverty in 1975-6 could have been eliminated if the aggregate supply position in regard to basic wage-goods was higher, let us say, about 25% to 30%, and Poverty would not raise its ugly head, if from 1975-76 onwards, each year our aggregate supplies of these goods would be growing at the same rate as our population would be growing. Thus, there is a basic wage-goods gap in the economy, which explains poverty.'[3]

Professor Tomlinson also acknowledged the nexus between poverty and the wage-goods 'gap'.

After the 1950s the world economy picked up and entered a 'golden age' but India missed the boat, underperforming the world average. It maintained a growth rate of 1.5 percentage points below the Third World average between 1950 and 1980. This was in part because India did not pursue free market policies and Nehru's socialist policies, critically termed 'Licence Raj', chained the economy down in unnecessary bureaucracy, thereby killing all entrepreneurial incentive to increase productivity and competitivity. Even under the Raj, where native incentives were likewise suppressed, business was much more fluid.

The point was proven when in the 1990s India changed tack in the 'Reform period' and reversed the Nehruvian economic

---

[3] Dr. BRAHMANANDA.

strategies. The effect was an almost instantaneous increase of growth. With the change in political economy came a change in mentality, in this case confidence. Those with a mind for business felt emboldened to take risks as the profits accrued would fall predominantly into their own hands and not those of the Leviathan state.

'One reason why India ranked ahead of China in 1700 of the past 2000 years was that the areas that today constitute Pakistan and Bangladesh were part of India. The British sliced off 20 percent of India's best wheat and rice growing areas. In the early 1940s, Jawaharlal Nehru said that after independence India would take its rightful place as a major world power. He was dead wrong. Due to the loss of important areas as Punjab and Sindh, independent India was born crippled at birth.'[4]

History has gone on to disprove the above comment as we have seen that what crippled India was policy and ineffective institutions, which rectified themselves in the 1990s.

The Raj has often been accused of having killed Indian self-confidence and such criticisms are not unfounded.

'The more damaging impact of colonialism may well have been to Indian minds – it created an inferiority complex from which they have only recently recovered.'[5]

What seems paradoxical is the moment that India finally had her first breath of freedom led by Nehru, she committed the

---

[4] SIMHA, Rakesh Krishnan, *'Forget Kohinoor, The British Looted Greater Treasures From India'*, www.swarajyamag.com (2016)
[5] DAS, Gurcharan, *India: How a rich nation became poor and will be rich again.*

same error of stifling India's entrepreneurs, knowing full well her recent history.

In the 1920s, there had at last been tariff protection for India, but it was a case of too little too late. Industrialisation did increase but it only employed a workforce of 2.5 million out of a population of 350 million. It was therefore mournfully insufficient to transform an agrarian society; a society, which had, in part, been kept that way to serve the economic interests of Britain. It also meant there would be a lack of effective demand for certain products as a poor population could not have afforded modern goods and services. This would naturally reduce the scope for business opportunities.

According to the economist Morris D. Morris, India had been unable to export such goods and services due to 'supply constraints', which meant they could not obtain the technology, labour skills or necessary finance, thereby increasing costs and reducing competivity in an international market. The historian Rajat Ray believed the chief impediment was the shortage of technological progress. Indian products were therefore less competitive to those of their international competitors. The question now was to what extent did the tariffs on Indian imports and the lack of effective training in India contribute to these factors?

The author and former CEO for Procter & Gamble India, Gurcharan Das, believes they could have imported such technologies as in the case of Tata, the steel producer, and Birla, the money lender turned jute manufacturer. But that is a bit like saying everyone can be a billionaire. In theory they can, of course, but in practice it turns out to be bit more difficult than that. In the case of G.D. Birla's business, had World War I not intervened he may not have been able to overcome the continuing obstacles placed before him by the British and predominantly Scottish merchants, who employed all manner of unethical and monopolistic tactics available to them.

As for the Tata company, Jamsetji Tata 'the father of Indian industry', chose to engage in an industry dominated by the British. After starting a trading company he invested his money in a series of mills and a year before his death opened India's first hotel with electricity, the Taj Mahal Hotel on the Colaba waterfront in Mumbai. His elder son and successor, Dorabji, started Tata Iron and Steel company (TISCO), which took the company onto the international stage with offices in London.

It is evident that while he may have been the object of British scorn for his efforts, he was not stopped by the Government of India. And had he not been singularly motivated, as he was by British underinvestment in India's industries and the subsequent poverty in his country, he may not have had the superhuman perseverance required to scale the mountain that he did.

It was India that had the *first* steel works in Asia thanks to Tata. And so India must have been ahead of the rest of Asia in terms of ideas and institutions, however occlusive they may have been. He did, after, all, visit England on several occasions and was educated at the British Elphinstone College of Mumbai. It was a lecture given by Thomas Carlyle in Manchester, while on a visit for mill machinery, which inspired him to set about constructing a steel plant. It would be his son Doab, who finally realised the project three years after his father's death and it would take a further five years before the first commercial ingot was produced in 1912. It is probably for these reasons that Das remarked,

'I do not think there was a British conspiracy to deliberately under-invest in India or sabotage Indian business interests... I believe the industrial revolution did not occur because Indian agriculture remained stagnant, and you cannot have an industrial revolution without an agricultural surplus or the means to feed a rapidly growing urban population.'[6]

British India did possess all the other elements necessary for commercial success at the time, namely: the rule of law, peace, a non-interventionist administration and essential infrastructures in the railways, telegraph and canals. The business elite would also have had a command of the English language, the *lingua franca* of world commerce, and therefore direct access to spheres of British trading influence, which were vast. In fact, Tata's first task, while still under his father's command was to set up company offices in Hong Kong, a British colony.

But there is still more to consider when reflecting on the historical roots of India's poverty and the role, if any, of British colonial policy in creating its modern occurrence.

The classical explanation for India's poverty is the fact that it has such a large population, which results in less jobs and opportunities. And tethered to that is the consequent reality that any progress in GDP is simultaneously swallowed up by an ever-expanding population. Between 1950 and 1980 economic growth was 3.5% while population growth was 2.2% therefore the net effect on income was only 1.3% per capita. This phenomenon is referred to as the 'Hindu rate of growth', as if cultural values or religion were somehow the cause. But it does not offer an answer. There are countries with greater population densities that are extremely prosperous. In 2010, according to

---

[6] DAS, Gurcharan, *India: How a rich nation became poor and will be rich again.*

the World Bank, India's population density was 412 per km² with a GNP per capita of \$3,300 while the Netherlands was 493 per km² with a GNP per capita of \$41,010. Hong Kong, likewise, had a population density of 6,783 per km² with a GNP per capita of \$48,170. So it is possible to sustain dense populations and be highly successful, especially considering Hong Kong's GNP per capita was 26% higher than Britain's, her former colonial master.

There is no association then between the two and this is further confirmed by sparsely populated areas that are rich, such as Australia and Canada, and those that are poor, in the case of Mozambique and Ethiopia.

In fact, densely populated areas are often the vehicles of prosperity as they concentrate people in cities and provide the means for industry and labour. This would explain why cities tend to be wealthier than rural areas, because there is a division of labour, i.e. specialisation, which leads to higher productivity, lower costs and is the basis for prosperity and higher incomes.

On Independence the Raj left India with an appalling illiteracy rate of 83%, especially for a coloniser with institutions back home of the calibre of Oxford and Cambridge. India, much to her credit, has taken up the baton. This lack of education of the average Indian (Britain has had basic education since 1870) is considered a source of India's poverty. Were this true there would have to be a clear correlation between high literacy and high incomes, but that is not what we see. In the region of Kerala, world famous now for its literacy rate of 94%, the Per Capita GDP in 2011 was 53,430 Rs, while the Haryana with a 77% literacy rate was 63,050 Rs.[7]

---

[7] SHAH, Parth J., *Why is India Poor?*, Centre for Civil Society - Liberty & Society Series 1 (Aug., 2013) p.19

A clearer illustration of this is comparing the higher literacy rate of Cubans as against the US. Lifting the embargo would raise living-standards radically, but it wouldn't put the country on a par with the US. So, a connection between literacy and economic performance is not a strict one, as there are other factors at work.

Perhaps, the most obvious reason is that of the colonial legacy, explicitly, the condition in which Britain left India, which was barley industrialised, illiterate and partitioned. Once more the issue refuses to follow a simple line of argument the very moment comparisons are made. Not all colonies are poor. There is Singapore, South Korea and Botswana that are prosperous and Zambia even had a higher GDP under colonial rule.

Then take the colonisers, they are not the richest amongst states in Europe. First Portugal and then Spain founded their colonies and the rest of Europe followed. They had their colonies the longest but they are not the wealthiest. But who are? As fate would have it, we see countries that never colonised anyone, namely Luxembourg and Switzerland, at the peak of European economic achievement. Maybe the Canadian economist Viner was right after all, and the colonies did eventually lose money for the colonisers. Luxembourg's GNP per capita is significantly higher than that of Britain's.

So colonialism is not an outright decisive factor of a country's contemporary economic state. Each case has to be judged on its own merits, analysing what each coloniser did in its colonies and the policies pursued by native governments on becoming independent.

Cultural aspects such as a lack of work ethic, which the British ruling India believed to be the case, are sometimes used to explain the lack of development. Climatic ones such as the enervating heat have also been proposed. However,

'Sir John Hick's Economic Principle does trump in most cases. It states that "people would act economically; when the opportunity of an advantage was presented to them they would take it." '[8]

How India responded to the Green Revolution in the 1960s and how Indians have performed abroad are clear examples of this theory in practice. Evidently, there was a better economic climate for them to act in. Therefore, cultural attitudes as a convenient catch-all explanation for poverty, do not match up either.

Gandhi was convinced that the source of India's poverty was the people's withholding of gold and silver from circulation.

'If [India] has for a hundred years exported more goods than she has received, it is because since the days of Pliny she has preferred to import gold rather than goods, and chosen to hoard her riches, or to congeal them into jewelry, rather than invest them in productive enterprise... and Sir Valentine Chirol has calculated that if the wealth thus hoarded during the last half-century had been liberated to finance and stimulate industry, the proceeds would now suffice to discharge the whole of India's public debt.'[9]

Perhaps one needs to look at the institutions and policies in place to find the answer. And in order to do this we need to find examples of twins separated at birth, that is, peoples of the same cultural background, education with access to equal

---

[8] DAS, Gurcharan, Essay - *India: How a rich nation became poor and will be rich again* (March 19, 2007) Author of *India Unbound*
[9] DURANT, p.170

resources tragically divided by fate and then placed upon very different economic paths. The most obvious example of such a country being divided in this way is Korea, with its communist North and capitalist South.

The differing economic political systems gave vastly different outcomes when it comes to prosperity. The per capita income of South Korea at the start of the 21st century was $19,614 whereas North Korea's has barely changed since the 1950s, at $1,122.

Korea is not alone in having undergone this natural simulation in practical economics. Germany was split after the war and Hong Kong was long disconnected from China. In the case of Hong Kong, immigrants fled across the border entering the British colony before the flood was stopped by the Chinese government. In effect people voted with their feet as to which system they preferred. And there was no democracy in either of the two. What Hong Kong did have was the rule of English law and economic opportunity.

In the case of Korea those in the North are kept, as was once the fate of all East Germans, behind walls, guarded by armed sentries and barbed wire. In each case the state that out-performed their stagnating and estranged twin was underpinned by its high degree of economic freedom.

'Individuals have economic freedom when property they acquire without the use of force, fraud or theft is protected from physical invasions by others and they are free to use, exchange, or give away their property as long as their actions do not violate the identical rights of others.'[10]

---

[10] SHAH, *Why is India Poor?* p. 28, James Gwartney, one of the principal editors of the Economic Freedom of the World Report

For this to be significant then, one should find a clear relationship between economic freedom and per capita GDP and that is precisely what one discovers.

'Population illiteracy, corruption, culture, democracy, and colonisation are, at best, half-truths. Institutions and policies determine economic success. The most important institutions and policies are those that enable... economic freedom!'[11]

What about India? We have seen the phenomenon of the 'Hindu rate of growth' but,

'Things began to change with modest liberalization in the eighties when annual economic growth rose to 5.6 per cent. This happy trend continued in the reform decade of the nineties when growth averaged 6.2% a year, while population slowed to 1.8%; thus, per capita income rose by a decent 4.4 per cent a year.'[12]

What changed was not the population or literacy levels, but rather the policies followed by institutions and it was this that led to an increase in opportunities.

Today we see similar beliefs being expressed from within Africa by her business people, blaming the economic difficulties faced in many quarters on the vast continent on unnecessary red tape. They call for the shackles of this stifling government bureaucracy to be removed. In freeing the people from such burdens it will enable all citizens to easily start their own business and keep most of the profit, which they will then in turn plough back into the local economy, benefitting many

---

[11] SHAH, Parth J., *Why is India Poor?* p.31
[12] DAS, Gurcharan, *India: How a rich nation became poor and will be rich again.*

more around them, rather than losing their surplus to the state where it is either siphoned off or poorly invested. While such red tape exists, as it once did in India, it will only suppress prosperity and encourage corruption, as those desperate to get ahead must bribe officials in order to circumvent the official hurdles placed before them.

Poverty is the default situation for all of human history, as Stepen Pinker is quick to point out. Prosperity is the exception and the miracle of our species. And yet we seem to spend more time on seeking out excuses for poverty, rather than learning the lessons of how to promote and foster prosperity.

In sum, we must concede that Britain is partially to blame for India's present poverty, as it was her policies that stunted India's industrialisation and reduced opportunity, but only in part. Industries were founded in India that competed directly with Britain and were not closed by the state. There were also conditions suitable to engender lucrative business, utilised above all by Tata and Birla. Finally, there came the much-belated state tariffs in the 1920s to protect India's fledgling industries. The other 'half' of the blame must lie with immediate post-Independence policies that shackled economic freedom and the 1930s hangover that so affected the rural poor.

'the historical roots of contemporary Indian poverty, in the form in which it has manifested itself in recent years, can be traced specifically to events in the agrarian economy of the inter-war years.'[13]

One could try and claim that Britain has been making up some of that difference by sending foreign aid (as atonement?)

[13] TOMLINSON, B.R., *The Historical Roots of Indian Poverty: Issues in the Economic and Social History of Modern South Asia: 1880-1960*, (Cambridge University Press, 1988) p.135

£283 million a year since 2011, but it is a fraction of the billions she received from India during the Second World War alone. In 2016, Britain's total foreign aid expenditure came in at £12.23 billion for the whole world.

> *'I have seen a great people starving to death before my eyes, and I am convinced that this exhaustion and starvation are due not, as their beneficiaries claim, to overpopulation and superstition, but to the most sordid and criminal exploitation of one nation by another in all recorded history.'*[14]

To what extent, though, was this visible state of poverty a recent occurrence brought on by the British and to what degree had it always been there?

One such oppressed section of the population that would have made an impression on any foreign visitor would have been the Dalits, the 'Untouchables', and on this subject Gandhi held nothing back,

> *'In the history of the world religions there is perhaps nothing like our treatment of the suppressed classes... Should we Hindus not wash our blood-stained hands before we ask the English to wash theirs.... India is guilty. England has done nothing blacker.'*[15]

But this scenario has not shifted with the sands of time. It is India that has cemented this belief into their society. In 2009, a High Court Judge on appeal had to overturn the original-trial judge's ruling for telling the defendant that, *"The dignity of a person of low integrity will not be lowered further in case his name*

---

[14] DURANT, pp.1-2
[15] ROLLAND, Romain, *Mahatma Gandhi* (New York, 1924) p.133

appears in a defamatory piece of news."[16] It shows how integrated this belief system really is, and at the same time gives due credit to the Indian judiciary system for having the maturity to rule against it.

'Low-caste Hindus remain subject to daily petty humiliations, police violence, rape and even murder, a major new report claimed.'[17]

It is estimated today that every 20 minutes a crime is committed against a Dalit. There are even murders of Dalits for 'daring' to drink from the same fountain as someone from a 'superior' caste or for a Dalit father complaining that his daughter has been raped. How do you rape someone without touching them? The former Indian Prime Minister, Dr. Manmohan Singh, referred to untouchability as a *'blot on humanity'*, echoing Gandhi's sentiments. It is a bit rich to place the blame for such an unparalleled state of affairs squarely at the feet of the British.

---

[16] 'Court ruling challenges India's caste system', *The Telegraph* (17 Mar., 2009)

[17] 'Caste system still blighting India', *The Telegraph* (14 Feb., 2007) Report by New-York based Human Rights Watch *'Research published last year from surveys in 565 villages showed that in 80 per cent of them old practices of untouchability endure'*, *'The Indian government's own figures show that Dalits are routinely brushed off by police and the courts when they try to seek justice. Between 1999 and 2001 some 89 per cent of trials for offences against Dalits resulted in acquittals.'*

CHAPTER
- V -
A PLACE IN INDIAN HISTORY

The British had based their 'legitimacy' for ruling India, in part, on the fact that they had saved India from despotic Mughal control, with its abuses, cruelties and extravagances. Its wanton luxury was a clear indicator of how divorced this 'foreign' presence was from its oppressed subjects. But was this really the case or was it little more than British propaganda?

It was true that there had been extremism during the reign of Emperor Aurangzeb when the English arrived, but there had also been greatness, in Akbar. And before the Mughals, there had even been both in the same man, in the 14th century Delhi Sultan Muhammad bin Tughla, known by some as 'Muhammad the Bloody', and yet:

'Both Barani and Ibn Batuta acknowledge the depth of royal concern and note the measures taken to relieve distress by distributing existing grain stocks and arranging imports from further afield. Subsequently, vast sums were disbursed to agents who undertook to bring wasteland into cultivation in an attempt to pre-empt future famines. This admirable initiative failed utterly. As Muhammad's reign degenerated into chaos, the agents pocketed the cash advances.'[1]

---

[1] Ibid., pp.268-9

But the question remains: were the Indians better off under the Mughals? From some comments made by observers such as the American writer Will Durant, one would say they clearly were, but a noted French observer during the time of the Mughals had this to say,

'In consequence the peasant's lot was not, even in good times, a happy one. François Bernier, a doctor who travelled widely in India in the 1660s and then reported his findings to Louis XIV's chief minister, described the lot of the Indian peasant as a 'debasing state of slavery.' '[1]

And while on the topic of slavery, the condition existed long before the British arrived in India. The British Raj tolerated it and it was more widespread than in the US and all of Britain's other colonies combined.

It is said by writers such as Tharoor that one cannot judge Islamic intervention in India by the same measure as the British, because the Muslims stayed and made India their home. However, before they finally settled down they had invaded, ransacked, desecrated temples time and again and left with untold booty. The British stayed from the first and one might say had the dignity to leave at the last. They also built an infrastructure that is still used to this day by the wider population. The Taj Mahal is an unrivalled thing of beauty but in the practical sense it doesn't help the average Indian get through the day, apart from those that have businesses in its immediate vicinity or work in the tourism industry. It was not built with the wider population in mind.

---

[1] KEAY, p.321

When it came to the economy, the British followed the Mughal lead in land revenue collection and the Mughal system was not a leaner burden than that of the British,

'The Mughal state was an insatiable Leviathan, its impact on the economy was defined above all by its unlimited appetite for resource.'[2]

There was clear evidence of Mughal riches,

'All foreign visitors to the India of the six great Mughals – Babur, Humayun, Akbar, Jahangir, Shah Jahan and Aurangzeb – found ample evidence of an awesome authority and were stunned by the magnificence of the imperial setting. This last was most obviously architectural but not exclusively. The eye-catching profusion of solid gold and chased silver, precious silks and brocades, massive jewels, priceless carpets and inlaid marbles was probably without parallel in history.'[3]

The Mughal state took, *'one-third of all foodgrain production and perhaps one-fifth of other crops.'*[4] And the same would occur under the British. But here the debate is how much was ploughed back into the country in services and infrastructure by the British and how much was spent on Mughal pomp and magnificence?

"If we take the period when the Mughul dominion – the most powerful rule in the two preceding centuries – was at its zenith, we find from contemporary writers that while there was a thin crust of splendour at the top, below were dense layers of squalor and misery and suffering.

---

[2] RAYCHAUDHURI, Tapan, 'The Mughal Empire', in 'The State and the Economy', *The Cambridge Economic History of India,* p.173
[3] KEAY, p.326
[4] RICHARDS, J.F., *The Mughal Empire etc.* p.63

Almost the sole surviving legacy of that epoch is the pathetic magnificence of palaces and temples and tombs."[5]

Akbar's imperial income for just one year amounted to £120,000,000. It was a *'sum at which contemporary Europe marvelled, and which we must consider in the light of the much greater purchasing power of money in the sixteenth century.'*[6]

If we multiply by 204 we reach today's figure and no sums mentioned thus far concerning British land revenue, Home Charges and the like, have come close to such an exorbitant annual sum.

However, the British administrator of Bengal, F.J. Shore, spoke in the House of Commons in 1857, testifying that, *"it has always been our boast how greatly we have raised the revenue above that which the native rulers were able to extort."*[7]

The Mughals had spent their wealth in the country and for that some commentators put them above the British, but what is the net worth left behind by the British in infrastructure, as well as the by-products of its linguistic legacy and political union? That is not to mention the money they also spent in the country on wages, works and permanent jobs created thereafter.

The *Pax Britannica* offered the sub-continent its first taste of sustained peace since the in-fighting of the Mughal successions. Under The Company and later the Crown, there would be no such internal conflict and the Indian population benefitted from this welcome peace. That was of course once all the British conquests had been carried out and the 1857 rebellion suppressed.

---

[5] CURZON, Lord, *The North American Review*, Vol. 192, No. 657 (Aug.,1910) p.155
[6] GARBE, Richard, 'Akbar Emperor of India. A Picture of Life and Customs from the Sixteenth century', *The Monist*,Vol. 19, No. 2 (April, 1909) p.177
[7] DURANT, p. 16-7

"Above all, we have given to India the priceless boon of peace instead of war, settled life in place of anarchy, security in place of brigandage and rapine."[8]

However, John Morley calculated that in the 19th century alone Britain had engaged in 111 wars within India, using for the most part Indian troops.[9]

One could say that if the Indian had had it so bad under British control then why was there not increased migration into the Princely states? There were over five hundred of them dotted all over India, an area of over two-fifths of the sub-continent. It would have been the closest thing to living in a 'Free India'. Many Chinese, for example, migrated into Hong Kong over the years to live in an undemocratic British colony because conditions were better there, despite its inadequacies.

'It does not appear that there is any considerable migration from the provinces directly under British dominion to those which are under native rule. The people, no doubt, are generally fixed to their habitations by poverty and difficulty of movement; still, if they greatly preferred the native rule, a certain amount of migration to it there would probably be.'[10]

For the British the bogey man that they preferred to compare themselves to was the fundamentalist Aurangzeb. He had also provoked ill-will among the Hindus with his temple destruction and restrictions on reconstruction.

---

[8] CURZON, Lord, *The North American Review*, p.154
[9] DURANT, p.14-5
[10] SMITH, Goldwin, 'British Empire in India', *The North American Review*, Vol. 183, No. 598 (Sep 7, 1906) p.346-7

But against Akbar they wisely dared not judge themselves. Few rulers carry the epithet of Great. England has only one: Alfred, and for the Mughals it was their third ruler, Akbar, the Great (1542-1605). He was a contemporary of Elizabeth I, who died just two years before him, but she was not his equal.

'In comparison with 'medieval' India, early modern England seems remarkably provincial.'[11]

At a time when England was still embroiled in religious turmoil and intolerance, Akbar had the wisdom and vision to tolerate all religions. He renounced his faith of Islam, after doubting the divine origin of the Koran, and distrusted any faith that proclaimed itself to be the sole possessor of the truth. Above all, he rejected *'the intolerant exclusiveness of Sunnitic Islam.'* He started a debating school for all denominations to openly challenge one another, the famous 1575 Ibadat Khana (House of Worship) in Agra, and thereby established a precedent for rationalism in India.

He opened schools for the Hindu and Muslim alike, despite being unable to read and write himself.

He assisted the farmer that made land arable by providing free seed and four years of reduced taxation.

The poll tax that had been imposed on Hindus was removed from the outset, despite the huge blow this would incur to the royal treasury.

He created a uniformed money system before the British did and achieved something even they shied away from and that was the outlawing of the Hindu tradition of child marriage,

---

[11] STEVENS, Paul, & SAPRA, Rahul, 'Akbar's Dream: Moghul Toleration and English/British Orientalism', *Modern Philology*, Vol. 104, No. 3 (February 2003) p.399

'that is to say the marriage of boys under sixteen and girls under fourteen years, and he permitted the remarriage of widows.' He also forbade *sati*, the practice of a widow throwing herself onto her husband's funeral pyre, declaring that it did not accord to Brahman custom. And did away with the Muslim prohibition of wine.

> *'Akbar succeeded in establishing order, peace, and prosperity in the regained and newly subjugated provinces. This he brought about by the introduction of a model administration, an excellent police, a regulated post service, and especially a just division of taxes.'*[12]

The list goes on, but it does depend on your persuasion. With time he grew weary of Islam asserting its superiority from the vantage point of the royal court. In the open debates in Agra presided by Akbar, the Ulemas, *'who had always put forward such great claims'*, were found wanting when placed under careful cross-examination. Later Akbar would consider the persistence of the Portuguese Jesuits, invited to his court, to try and convert him more troublesome than the Ulemas. In 1580, Akbar founded his own all-encompassing religion to bring all faiths in under one roof, *Din i Ilahi*, 'the religion of God'. He grew further apart from Islam, going as far as to ban the use of Arabic and pushed Arabic books to one side in the imperial library. Nevertheless, he granted universal freedom of worship and in that *'he placed all men on an equality without regard to race or religion.'* To the Christians he gave them the autonomy to build churches and proselytize; to the Sikhs he gave the city of Amritsar; to the Jains he gave shelter and to the Hindus he gave his time and dedication in relieving them of previous burdens

---

[12] GARBE, p.171

and recovered their traditions. But for many visiting Europeans they perceived this religious tolerance as *'confusion'*.

> *'when in the Occident... many bloody persecutions occurred from time to time; when in the Occident men were imprisoned, executed or burnt at the stake for the sake of their faith or their doubts; at a time when Europe was polluted by the horrors of witch-persecution and the massacre of St. Bartholemew. Under Akbar's rule India stood upon a much higher plane of civilization than Europe at the same time.'*[13]

Akbar ensured his sons had both Christian and Muslim tutors so that they would form independent views from *'the comparison of contrasts'*. But his sons would be a great disappointment to him, and none more so than Aurangzeb (1618-1707), the sixth Mughal ruler, who undid the best part of all Mughal rule in India. In a world still struggling for peace on earth, which can only come through tolerance between religions, Akbar was a man ahead of his time.

No, the British decided not to mention Akbar's reign when it came to legitimising their own.

> *'Not only did the British give India a legal system, an efficient police force, an apolitical army and a smooth running - if astonishingly bureaucratic - civil service, but just look at the concrete benefits they provided.'*[14]

---

[13] Ibid., p.200

[14] PRESTON, John, *The British were imperialist Brutes? No, Britain made India great (says an Indian!)*, MailOnline (17 Mar., 2016) – Book review of *The Making of India: The Untold Story of British Enterprise* by Kartar Lalvani

CHAPTER
- VI -

THE INDIAN RENAISSANCE

Britain did not just supply India with purely tangible benefits but the colonising country also contributed in the intangible spheres of knowledge and education. The Indian Renaissance, namely the religious and social reform of the early 19th century, was brought about in great part due to Western ideas brought into India. Ideas that were not just European but British also. The leaders of the Free India Movement had all spent time in Europe, but above all in Britain. Why did they not go east to China? They instead travelled West because Europe was where the ideas were, and the sort of future India wanted for herself.

Gandhi was in the main dismissively one-sided concerning most things from the West, which was hypocritical of the sort of snobbery he accused the British of when they belittled the East. That said, he had thought British government was in the main good, but he was referring to the government that was enjoyed by the people in Britain, not its truncated form applied in India.

The central figure in this awakening in India, which could have happened before but did not occur until the British arrived, was Raja Rammohan Roy. Roy was the man that helped William Bentinck pass the 1829 law forbidding *sati*, which was the first successful social movement against an age-old custom. Roy also propagated Western education, seeing it as a tool for spreading modern ideas through India. He maintained an English school in Calcutta and established Vedanta College, offering Indian and Western learning in social and physical science. He even petitioned the government for wider education in English.

There were other notable humanists such as Keshah Chandra, Iswar Chandra, Debendranath Tagore, the Indo-Portuguese Derozio, the saint Ramakrishna Paramhamsa, Govindrao Phule, Syed Ahmad Khan, and the Irish woman Annie Besant among others, not forgetting to mention the many organisations that came together to push for progress. They all worked tirelessly to break down the barriers of the caste system; defend the rights of women, especially the remarriage of widows; abolish the practice of purdah, which was the screening of women from men or strangers, especially by means of a curtain; modernise religious beliefs through invigorating scholarship, and called for general social reform for the oppressed. Once again Britain was the unintentional catalyst, while the Indians were the active protagonists.

'The total number of public hospitals and dispensaries under the control of the Imperial government of India was about 1200 in 1880 and in 1902, the figure raised to approximately 2500. There was one hospital for every 330 square miles in 1902. The income of public health facilities was 3.6 million rupees in 1880 and about 8.1 million rupees in 1902. Patient turnover was 7.4 million in 1880; that increased to about 22 million in 1902.'[1]

The Lady Hardinge Medical College was also established in 1916 by the Viceroy's wife for Indian women to study medicine.

The Indian Medical Service efficiently cleared up deadly epidemics like the plague and cholera. Almost all the diseases

---

[1] Government of India. New ed., published under the authority of His Majesty's secretary of state for India in council. Vol. IV Administrative. Oxford: Clarendon Press; 1909. *The Imperial Gazetteer of India*; pp. 457–80.

prevalent at that time in India like small pox, leprosy, and malaria were successfully controlled, though, epidemics did still come and go.

> *'There were also marked improvements in public health, which increased Indian life expectancy by eleven years.* '*[2]

Gandhi despised western medicine, but even he eventually succumbed to it when he needed to be operated upon for an appendicitis in 1924. But of course, one must consider how much of western medicine is indebted to the Arab world, which is a great deal, so it is not such a radical break with the East. Medieval Arab medicine was quite clearly the dawn of modern western medical treatment.

The British introduced quinine as an anti-malarial defence which the Britishers took to mixing with gin and diluting with Indian tonic water, thus giving birth to the ubiquitous G&T. The prevalence of the disease in India becomes apparent when one learns of Sitla, the goddess of smallpox, and the surprising fact that she is worshipped by both Hindus and Muslims out in the countryside.[3]

The British also did their best to eradicate thuggee - the organised gangs of professional robbers and murderers, who also sold children into slavery. They successfully tackled dacoity, as well, which was banditry, and not forgetting the practice of *sati*. General Sir Charles Napier had pushed aside the relativism of cultural disparities and promised to act according

---

[2] FERGUSON, Niall, *Empire – How Britain Made the World*, p.216 (Ferguson's footnote: **From 21 years to 32. However, in the same period (between 1820 and 1950), British life expectancy increased from 40 to 69 years.)*

[3] STEVENS, Paul, & SAPRA, Rahul, 'Akbar's Dream: Moghul Toleration and English/British Orientalism', *Modern Philology*, Vol. 104, No. 3 (February 2003) p.401

to the custom of his own country when he said, *'when men burn women alive we hang them.'* However, this negates the indispensable role played by the major campaign undertaken by the Indian Raja Rammohan Roy, 'the father of the Indian Renaissance'. The British, as we have seen, tended to leave local customs alone. They could have tackled child marriage, but chose not to, going as far as overturning the Indian decision in Congress to raise the age. So, without Roy's campaign, one could say the British may not have even taken the necessary steps to ban *sati*. The Portuguese also eradicated the practice, and did it 309 years ahead of the British.

> *'In legislation upon matters of social reform the Indian Government has always thrown its weight upon the side of the status quo... The bill to raise the age of consent was resisted by the Government for many years; the bill for universal primary education was defeated by the Government in 1911 and in 1916.'*[4]

The British also contributed to the recording of the history of India. Captain James Tod was the historian of Rajputana and the Rajputs in his *Annals and Antiquities of Rajas'han* as well as *Travels in Western India*. It was the Asiatic Society that notoriously discovered the links between Indian and European languages under William Jones and James Grant Duff, who was also the first historian of the Marathas.

> *'It was European scholars, chiefly English, who studied the languages and cultures of ancient India, and resurrected Vedic literature and wisdom; it was Europe that revealed India*

---

[4] DURANT, p.189

to the Hindus.'[5]

Western thought was integrated into India, despite Gandhi's opinion on being asked what he thought about Western civilisation and replying, *"It would be a nice thing."* Such Western learning has connected India to the wider western-influenced world and its fundamental rationalism. Such scientific logic is a Western mainstay. Tie this to the acceptance of English as the argot of national unity and the pairing has led India to lend her voice to the wider global community like never before. Her students travel abroad and integrate seamlessly into the international workplace, her professors take up important posts teaching international students, while her writers occupy centre stage in the literary world.

It does not mean to say that the English language is in some way an inherently better language than another, which some native speakers may like to presume. It is not as logical as Esperanto and does not possess the musicality of Swahili , nor is it as pleasing to the ear as French, Italian or even Russian. It is merely a unifying language and *any* language can fulfil that important role.

Not only is English the language of business and education, but it is also the language of navigation, aviation and tourism. India, therefore, does not have just *any* political language to hand, but rather *the* language that will ensure easier integration into the international community and grease the cogs of commerce. But, of course, this is yet another positive that was never a British design and therefore something the British cannot take conscious credit for. It has been suggested by some that Hindi fits the unifying bill for India perfectly and that there

---

[5] DURANT, p.175

is no need for English, but Hindi is missing the international dimension, which is already paying the country dividends as well as the political fact that English gives no group within India the political and cultural upper hand.

- VII -

RACE & EQUALITY

The unpublished memoir of an Irish lawyer, Manus Nunan, who was usually scathing about the English, contains nothing but praise for the District Officers he met in Nigeria during the 1950s: *'Their concern for the native people they governed was wonderful.'* The same would have been true for District Officers in India. E.D. Morel (1873-1924), a pacifist and politician, made the same point: such civil servants were *'strong in their sense of justice, keen in their sense of right, firm in their sense of duty'.* They were honest, doughty, responsible and, above all, industrious. But there were plenty of examples where precisely the opposite was true.

Even George Orwell, who had criticised much of Empire as *'a despotism with theft as its final object'*, believed the British strain of empire to be better than any other European variant.

According to campaigners there are up to 10,000 'honour killings' in India every year. Most of the victims are young women killed by their fathers and brothers over 'forbidden' relationships or for insisting on marrying a man they love.[1]

The majority of such killings occur in the north of the country and affect those marrying within their own sub-caste, which for those concerned with this long-standing custom of abstention considered akin to incest. Sometimes even rewards are offered

---

[1] *Indian caste councils praise families that carry out 'honour killings'*, The Telegraph (15 Jan., 2013)

by caste councils for a couple's murder, when they have rejected arranged marriages in favour of someone they love. Western liberal ideals still have a long way to go before they are widely   accepted.

'Researchers analysed the DNA of 132 individuals with wide-ranging backgrounds from 25 diverse groups around India. They found evidence of strong inbreeding leading to genetic groups that had been isolated from each other for thousands of years... The research challenges the notion that India's notorious rigid caste system, with its priestly Brahmans and low-status 'untouchables', was largely manufactured by the British.'[1]

This therefore undermines the notion from some historians that the caste system was not hereditary and it was much more flexible before the British arrived, who used the system for their purposes of divide and rule.

' "India is genetically not a single large population, but instead is best described as many smaller isolated populations," said Dr. Lalji Singh, one of the study leaders from the Centre for Cellular and Molecular Biology in Hyderabad.'[2]

Under British rule, though, it was clearly a case of all humans being equal with some more equal than others. Indians were not on a level footing with Europeans under the law, nor in opportunities in the bureaucracy. This is not the image the British are trying to claim today, and the British Raj was an endemically racist regime, but then so was Indian society at this

---

[1] *India's caste system 'is thousands of years old'*, DNA shows, The Telegraph (24 Sep., 2009)
[2] Ibid.

time with its caste system the rigid embodiment of that attitude. As for the British there was no more anecdotal symbol of their racism than the sign on the Royal Simla Club, which all Indians are familiar with and read *'Royal Simla Club – No Dogs or Indians.'*

In 1883, under Viceroy Ripon the tilted balances of justice had to be righted and the Ilbert Bill was passed to enable Indian judges to preside over cases involving Europeans. The Bill was incendiary, provoking what some called a 'White Mutiny' as the European community, predominantly the British, of Calcutta expressed their displeasure vocally and violently until it was eventually revoked.

With such emasculation came the spawning of the INC, Indian National Congress. The press campaign against the bill had seen an insidious outpouring of racist sentiment, which unwittingly united all of India's multifarious peoples, classes, castes and religions. The one thing all Indians had in common was their skin colour and the ruling elite had left them in no doubt that that was the dividing difference. Two members from the initial INC meeting would create the leaders that would later carry India to independence. One was Nehru, India's first Prime Minister, and the other was Subhas Chandra Bose, who openly engaged the British on the battlefield and also sought assistance, first from Hitler and then Japan to oust the British.

British law had had a chance to be the levelling force it has always claimed it was, but the Ilbert episode clearly showed it was nothing of the sort. The relevance of the issue was such that it spelt the end of the rule of the Raj. The thin veil of an honourable law code that would defend the equality of the native Indian was finally lifted, and no amount of executive hyperbole would replace it. It was the point of no return and it pushed the Nationalist movement across the Rubicon - *Alea iacta est.*

In two hundred years of British law only three Englishmen were ever executed for murdering an Indian, while thousands of Europeans, who had murdered Indians, went unpunished.

'An Englishman who shot dead his Indian servant got six months' jail time and a modest fine (then about 100 rupees) while an Indian convicted of attempted rape against an Englishwoman was sentenced to 20 years of rigorous imprisonment.'[3]

The British claim of having brought equality under the law, would only be achieved the moment they left. For while they remained, there could be no justice for the Indian in an authoritarian state. It does not pass unnoticed that for India to benefit from Britain, the British first would have to step aside.

---

[3] THAROOR, Shashi, 'Inglorious Empire': India strikes back', *The Irish Times*

CHAPTER

- VIII -

POLITICAL FRANCHISE

Democracy is another 'gift' claimed by the British despite there being no such representation in India during their rule.

'It is a bit rich to oppress, torture, imprison, enslave, deport and proscribe a people for 200 years, and then take credit for the fact that they are democratic at the end of it.'[1]

Some in India today believe a presidential system would better suit the nation. They bemoan the legacy of their antiquated penal code as well as the fact that they chose a parliamentary system in imitation of the British model. But India's founding fathers took their time, they didn't just follow the British form of democracy for convenience. The parliamentary system is the most popular democratic system in the world, for the obvious reason that it works best. How many states in the world have presidents and are falling apart or are riddled with the sort of corruption that has stagnated the economy? A parliamentary system allows for the easier removal of ineffective leaders and depends on a cabinet to make decisions, not the personality of an individual.

In fact, anyone that has read anything of the history concerning the Free Indian Movement becomes aware at once of the struggle for representation and a say in the decision making of their own country. There was no democracy for India while

---

[1] THAROOR, Shashi, 'Inglorious Empire': India strikes back', *The Irish Times*

the British were in power, just as there was no democracy in the British colony of Hong Kong. Only when Hong Kong was going to be handed back to China in 1997 did the British rapidly force through changes to give it some reputable veneer of autonomy, much to the annoyance of the Chinese government.

It was not as though London was unacquainted with the notion of increasing representation in its colonies as the Durham Report clearly showed in 1839. The report suggested that Canada be given,

'A system of responsible government [such] as would give the people a real control over its own destinies... The government of the colony should henceforth be carried on in conformity with the views of the majority in the Assembly.'[1]

The report was eventually put into effect, in fits and starts, and by 1856 most of the Canadian colonies had been granted their local self-government. Australia and New Zealand also followed in the same vein in the 1850s.

No such concessions were forthcoming for India though. What this meant was that the predominantly 'white' colonies would be shown due respect, while those at racial variance with the ruling nation would remain firmly under the British yoke. *'If India could not achieve its freedom like Canada it would take it like the United States.'*

The timing of the implementation of the Durham Report is crucial to our story here. It was not much before the Mutiny occurred in 1857. If the findings had also been applied in India, Britain's most important possession no less, while it would not have affected the rumours circling about animal fat and

---

[1] FERGUSON, Niall, p.111

cartridges that sparked the rebellion, it may have carried some sway over the ruling elites joining the rebellion and fanning the flames. In so doing, the retribution the British meted out in its wake would not have occurred and consequently the world would not have witnessed the depths of depravity that such a colonial power could stoop to.

They were the sort of atrocities that the administration had always maintained were characteristic of eastern despots, when promoting their 'civilised' British administration.

CHAPTER
- IX -

INTERFERENCE

India has kept her old ways. They were not destroyed by the British. Yes, the British involved themselves in eradicating such local practices as *sati* and thuggee, but ancient India is still alive and well. If *Hindutva* (preserving the ancient Hindu civilisation) is important to those Hindu nationalists that despise Britain's involvement in their country, which is a reasonable sentiment on the past, then they should be able to acknowledge that the colonial power left India's great heritage intact when it departed. The same, cannot be said for Europe after the Roman Empire swept through and eradicated whole peoples, customs and their languages, for example.

In the sphere of religion Britain did not proselytize nor force conversion as had happened in Portuguese Goa. The British did try to spread Christianity under the Crown, albeit in a less forceful manner. And they did attempt to spread The Word in one of the most underhanded ways, during the famines, hence the creation of the 'Rice Christians', those that converted for the sake of relieving the torment of hunger pangs. But how much headway could a new religion make in a land where Hinduism had been established for millennia? Only the Dalits had the most to gain by embracing the new religion as it gave them access to education and equality.

When Britain departed India her ancient Hindu civilisation was still preserved, as it is today.

CHAPTER

- X -

EDUCATION

India's ancient universities and gurukulas were world renowned, attracting foreign students in significant numbers. Most, including the ancient Nalanda University, were destroyed by Islamic conquerors, however, the country's schooling system continued as before. Dharampal explained in his 1983 book *The Beautiful Tree – Indigenous Indian Education in the Eighteenth Century* how the lower castes constituted the majority of students in Tamil Nadu, United Provinces and Bihar.

The British dismantled this egalitarian education system by destroying the guilds that financed these schools. And as Gandhi said, *"instead of taking hold of things as they were, began to root them out. They scratched the soil and began to look at the root, and left the root like that, and the beautiful tree perished."* Then they replaced it with a farce by contemporary UK standards. Angus Maddison explains:

'The education system which developed was a very pale reflection of that in the UK. Three universities were set up in 1857 in Calcutta, Madras and Bombay, but they were merely examining bodies and did no teaching. Higher education was carried out in affiliated colleges which gave a two-year B.A. course with heavy emphasis on rote learning and examinations.'[1]

---

[1] MADDISON, Angus, *The Economic and Social Impact of Colonial Rule in India. Chapter 3 of Class Structure and Economic Growth: India & Pakistan since the Moghuls* (1971), p.6

The claim that Britain put India on to the road of educational enlightenment is a bold but clearly frail assertion.

'The total expenditure for education in India is less than one-half the educational expenditure in New York State.'[1]

At the village level the programme put forward by the British was completely untenable, as no impoverished nation like India could afford such an expensive system. The tree was left to rot. Therefore:

'Britain's main failure was not to educate the Indian masses – hence 83% were illiterate at Independence.'[2]

---

[1] DURANT, p.46
[2] DAS

CHAPTER
- XI -
GRATITUDE

If anyone has ever seen the changing of the guard on the India-Pakistan border at Wagah, they will see that the ceremony is the same on both sides of the divide and the British influence is all too evident in both armed forces.

There is no questioning the fact that the British established the Indian army. But she cannot take credit for instilling her men with courage or fighting spirit, as India's history of over 3,000 years bears a bounty of evidence for such capacity. In fact, the Sikhs almost defeated the British in open battle on more than one occasion, and not every battle that the British waged across the sub-continent, despite its superior firepower and tactics, went their way.

It is patent that the Indian army was created to enforce British rule, while also ensuring imperial hegemony elsewhere in the world. Nowhere is this more felt than in the two World Wars where India's sacrifice and contribution has shamefully gone unrecognized back in Britain.

To put the record straight, the logistics for India's contribution in the Great War were colossal:

'She contributed at once $500,000,000 to the fund for prosecuting the War; she contributed $700,000,000 later in subscriptions to war loans; and she sent to the Allies various products to the value of

$1,250,000,000. The suspension of the Revolutionary movement enabled England to reduce the Indian army to 15,000.'[1]

The contribution in manpower was no less impressive totalling 1,338,620, which was 178,000 more than all the combined troops sent by Britain's white dominions of Australia, Canada, New Zealand and South Africa.[2] And even then Britain, shamelessly, could not keep her side of the bargain and grant India increased freedom and representation in her government after their unfailing support.

In 1918, Dr. Rutherford, a member of Parliament in Westminster, gave rent to his disgust over the Montagu-Chelmsford Reforms intended to make amends for India's deficient political arrangements,

'Never in the history of the world was such a hoax perpetrated upon a great people as England perpetrated upon India, when in return for India's invaluable service during the War, we gave to the Indian nation such a discreditable, disgraceful, undemocratic, tyrannical constitution.'[3]

It would be frustration over this betrayal that would lead to the Jallianwala Bagh massacre.

The Second World War saw a similarly dishonourable Déjà-vu treatment, but by then the die was cast.

The decision to back Britain during the Second World War was fraught with polemic for the Nationalist cause but Gandhi was persuaded on the explicit promise by the British government that it would earn India her independence.

---

[1] DURANT, pp.123-4
[2] Ibid., p.124
[3] THAROOR, Shashi, *An Era of Darkness: The British Empire in India* (2006) p.75

India thus provided 2.5 million men, which was the largest volunteer force in history. In monies received, Britain owed £1.3 billion, an eighth of British GDP. The war left 90,000 Indian soldiers dead, 6,000 sailors lost, 1,400 civilians killed by Japanese bombing. Half a million Indians also fled Burma, where perhaps one in ten perished. This part of British history is also another enigma for the British public and even for those that take more than just a passing interest in World War II.

During that war the Indian army exacted upon Japan what the Japanese consider their biggest ever defeat: the 1944 battle of Imphal and Kohima, which stifled Japan's attempt to invade India. The conflict, which saw 53,000 Japanese die out of an 85,000 strong invasion force, has even been referred to by some military historians as *'one of the fiercest battles in world history.'* And the imperial Japanese army inflicted arguably the most humiliating defeat ever suffered by a British army when they overran them in Singapore.

With all of this in mind, it probably came as no surprise when the writer and Indian MP Shashi Tharoor on a visit to London observed that, while there was even a war memorial to a dog, there was no such statue honouring the Indian soldiers that had made the ultimate sacrifice. Nor was there even a memorial to charitable India for her evident and, one could say, pivotal role in Britain's successful participation in the conflict.

As recently as 2011, the cargo ship S.S. Gairsoppa, which was sunk on 17th February 1941 by a German U-boat off the coast of Ireland, was found with its store of silver bullion. The shipment of 2,792 silver bars, or 3 million troy ounces of silver, was valued at £38,272,000 today. It was being carried to Britain to augment its dwindling war coffers after Britain had called in emergency supplies. In fact, the Empire as a whole donated

£23.3 million in gifts and £10.7 million in interest-free loans to boost the Allied war effort. The rescue of the bullion was the deepest recovery in history with the salvage company keeping 80% of the find with the other 20% going to the Royal Mint. It should, one would think, have been returned to India, but that would have broken with British tradition, looting right up until the present, one could say.

To put this historical trend of British covetousness into perspective, a Portuguese ship, the *Bom Jesus*, that sunk in 1533 was found on Namibia's notorious Skeleton coast in 2016. It had been carrying, among other valuable artefacts, gold coins currently valued at $13 million. The ship had been sailing from Lisbon en route to India and the gold was, therefore, not loot nor the property of the Indians in their Goan colony. The coins along with ivory and copper were to have been used to purchase Indian wares for sale in Europe. Portugal had a right to the treasure, as it was a ship of state, however, the Portuguese generously waived their right to the fortune allowing Namibia to keep it all.

It is not as if Portugal could spare the cash at the time, but the African country arguably needed it more. For Britain, though, the moral lesson was served.

Taken together, the points concerning India's contribution to Britain's war effort, one is left with the impression that had India not been involved, Britain's participation in two world wars, could have had very different outcomes, not only on the battle field but in her current account.

CHAPTER
- XII -

UNIFICATION

When Indian Nationalist commentators correct the claim that Britain is responsible for having created one nation, there is a grain of truth to this; it created three. But it is still contentious to claim that India (what the British left of it) would naturally exist today as a unified state with a common law and common infrastructure. Rather, it could so easily have carried on as a plethora of competing states, as in Europe. And the European ideal of democracy, which many of India's leaders experienced by visiting Britain, may never have materialised, or certainly not to such a full extent.

Tharoor believes that India would eventually have unified like Italy. That is indeed a confident prophecy. There are such things as experts on the past and experts on the present, but there is no such thing as an expert on the future. India could quite easily have become the Balkans but on a much grander scale. Italy, herself, was created on the back of three revolutions and three civil wars over 50 years and already possessed a European perspective and institutions. Was this the route Tharoor envisaged India would take?

If India woke on the day of their hard won independence and embraced democracy without bloodshed, it was because Britain had put everything in place in terms of political infrastructure and European ideals, even though, she never went through with allowing Indians political franchise. She, therefore, led India to the front door, only to keep her shut out until the hinges gave way under the force of protest. The integration of the 565 Princely States under a unified Indian flag was a joint British-Indian achievement brokered by Lord Mountbatten, Sardar Vallabhbhai Patel and V. P. Menon.

Even though India had been unified on several occasions in her illustrious past, there never was a lasting union and it was ruled for the benefit of an empire in each case. Admittedly, it is still an impressive fact that it occurred more than just once, over such a vast area and as early as the Mauryan civilisation in the fourth century BC. But the Mughal project was already tiltering when the British were there, undermined by a new power block, namely the Marathas. So, it is not as if the Mughal cohesion was ambushed by the British and an inevitable modern state of a unified India would have naturally followed.

A British staff officer of the 19th Indian Division observed as he drove to capture Rangoon,

'Twenty races, a dozen religions, a score of languages passed in those trucks and tanks. When my great-grandfather first went to India there had been many nations: now there was one – India.'[1]

By 1947 this was only a partial truth as India fractured into three. But perhaps the Second World War had more to do with forging an Independent India than is formally recognised and why Jinnah, leader of the All-India Muslim League, had said that the *"war which nobody welcomed proved to be a blessing in disguise."* The war had, after all, rendered independence unavoidable through the internal strife brought on by the doubling of prices, the obdurate quashing of dissent, the

---

[1] RAGHAVAN, Dr. Srinath, *India's War: World War II and the Making of Modern South Asia* (Basic Books, 2016)

requisitioning of manpower and goods, as well as the mobilisation and militarisation of Indian society. Add to that flammable concoction the already divisive methods emplaced by the British to stage-manage India's sectarian partitions and you naturally have an irredeemable crisis.

It is to Indian credit that they forged a democracy. The country could have fallen apart and the princes returned to their autonomous princedoms. Britain may have built a chassis for a democracy to run on but there was no experienced driver and the engine had never been tested.

Alfred Russell Wallace, the naturalist and co-discoverer of the theory of evolution through natural selection, wrote *The Wonderful Century* in 1899, a summary of what Britain had achieved during the previous 100 years. In his conclusion, however, he said Britain had treated *'the subject races'* with *'a strange mixture of good and evil.'*

The British did for India what the Belgians did for Rwanda by supporting one minority over a majority and thereby gaining their unrestricted cooperation. The Belgians favoured the Tutsi over the Hutu, following the German precedent who had colonised the kingdom before Belgium arrived in 1922. The British chose the Muslim over the Hindu. It also had the same catastrophic effect once the colonisers abandoned the countries.

'The creation and perpetuation of Hindu-Muslim antagonism was the most significant accomplishment of British imperial policy: the project of divide et impera would reach its culmination in the horrors of Partition that eventually accompanied the collapse

of British authority in 1947.'[2]

As early as 1859 the Governor of Bombay, Lord Elphinstone, had said that *"Divide et impera was the old Roman maxim, and it should be ours."*

But Gandhi had said, *"We divide and you rule."* Muslim-Hindu relations had never been easy before the British arrived. The Muslims had also arrived on the back of conquest and had occupied the high ground before the British displaced them. There are Indian intellectuals that believe Hindus were responsible for much of the ill-will between the two faiths leading up to Partition, but this does not in any way diminish the catalytic role played by the British. Simply put, had the British not appeared in India then Partition would never have occurred, but then neither would have the union.

The Muslim League had even accepted the 1946 Cabinet Mission plan, proposing a confederate India in three dominions but it was Nehru's Hindu Congress that rejected this last desperate effort. Why then the Congress party went on to sign the eventual partition is a mystery unless they too felt it was no longer possible to live side by side with Muslims, and yet there are 160 million Muslims living in India today. So, who gained from Partition?

"The tragedy of Partition, wrote Bombay-based writer Saadat Hasan Manto, was not that there were now two countries instead of one but the realisation that "human beings in both countries were slaves -

---

[2] THAROOR, Shashi, 'But what about the railways...? The myth of Britain's gifts to India', *The Guardian* (8 March 2017)

slaves of bigotry, slaves of religious passions, slaves of animal instincts and barbarity."[3]

All were to blame, but ultimately none more so than the British that had sowed the first seed of division, starting the Muslims on the path that would end with their insistence on an independent homeland. Few events from history beckon the reader to jump on to the page and scream "Stop!", telling the British not to entertain such a notion; telling the Hindus not to listen to the British. In the end who benefitted from it? The million that lost their lives? The survivors scarred by the terrifying inhumanity meted out? The two nations locked in an embittered struggle today? The area at risk of nuclear war? The British, who may have hoped to maintain a geopolitical foothold via Pakistan for assisting in help found their nation?

Partition saw the displacement of 6 million Sikhs, 92 million Muslims and 255 million Hindus. Lahore had been a cosmopolitan and Sikh centre, but not today. Initially there was no law saying people had to leave, many Muslims stayed on in India but as the sectarian violence spiralled out of control the situation became untenable for others to avoid the wave of terror as murder, rape and pillage became daily occurrences. Hell held no horror beyond that experienced during Partition.

The Raj had created the climate, like parents favouring one sibling over another, only to stand back and let the frustration between the two groups run its natural course.

'No greater indictment of the failure of British rule in India, can be found than the tragic manner of its end.'[4]

---

[3] DARYMPLE, William, 'The Great Divide – The Violent Legacy of Indian Partition', *The New Yorker* (2015) quoting Bombay-based writer Saadat Hasan Manto,

In the end the belief that a nation should be delineated according to religious beliefs, proved to be hollow for many, as over 5.8 million Pakistanis and 5.4 million Bangladeshis would eventually leave the nascent nation to carry on their lives among the religiously divergent states of Europe, thus proving that one's allegiance is first, and foremost, to the well-being of family rather than the worship of any god.

A recent survey from Islamabad has said that today 27% of its population is ready to live abroad, citing opportunities as the main reason and not just the recent rise in violence.[5]

Is India perhaps not learning any lessons from its colonial history and becoming the very thing it says it loathed during British rule? Take the demolition of the Babri Masjid mosque in 1992, for instance and the outpouring of religious intolerance. It lead to the death of 2,000 people during the inter-communal riots in the months that followed. Then there's the lack of investment in education and health care and even the need to plead for the rich to donate land to safeguard the poor against famine. It sounds as if little has changed since Independence. Some celebrate India overtaking Britain in terms of world GDP, but this only masks over the salient point of the wealth of the average Indian, which we have seen has some way yet to go.

And as for the economic miracle and upsurge in India's financial fortunes, this is due to the nation embracing angloglobalisation. To throw out the English language now as a medium for communication, as some Nationalists have called for, would be a death blow to an embryonic industrial nation and a case of cutting off your nose to spite your face. And

---

[4] THAROOR, Shashi, 'Inglorious Empire': India strikes back', *The Irish Times*
[5] YUSUF, Huma, 'Quit Pakistan Syndrome': A Country Loses Faith in Itself, article on newrepublic.com (June 18, 2011)

India's new found national pride would take on all the worst manifestations of insular bigotry, no better than the attitudes of her colonial masters.

It was claimed throughout the time of the Raj and for a century after by apologists that things would have been worse for India under another ruler. If the British had not arrived then it would have been the Russians. It has always been a safe rebuttal as it cannot be tested. It is also an especially self-assured piece of rhetoric, drawing as it does on decades of anti-Soviet prejudice.

Even Karl Marx made this point of India being better off under Britain than any other. He believed the British, through their railways, would usher in an industrial revolution and bring with it wholesale improvements for the labouring classes; he was wrong. And perhaps all those that insisted that India would have fared worse under Russia were also equally mistaken. It is one of the great questions from history, the *'what if'* scenario. But perhaps we do know a likely outcome of Russian intervention in India, if not the manner with which she may have ruled, by looking at how Russia left some of her colonies when they wrestled free from her iron grip,

'Now compare British colonialism with that of Russia. When Russia dissolved the Soviet Union in 1991 and set free its 14 republics, these newly independent countries had 100 percent literacy, thriving universities and robust industrial clusters. Ukraine was an agrarian basket case in the 1920s but by 1991 it had the crown jewels of Russian heavy industry. Kazakhs used to be nomads; Kazakhstan is a space power. Uzbekistan produces commercial airliners and military aircraft. The Central Asian republics, which did not even have a script

for their languages prior to the arrival of the Russians, became civilizationally uplifted. Inter-marriage among Russians and non-Russians was common in all the republics.'[6]

---

[6] SIMHA, Rakesh Krishnan, 'Forget Kohinoor, The British Looted Greater Treasures From India', (2016) https://swarajyamag.com

CHAPTER
- XIII -

NOT CRICKET

One final, undeniable, benefit of British rule, despite the majority Scottish workforce in the Indian Civil Service, was the introduction of cricket.

For those that love the game, and there are more in India than England, it is unfathomable as to why every nation on earth has not fallen in love with the well-loved sport and has instead fallen into the arms of football. Perhaps this could be a joint venture for Britain and India to embark upon in the future. But once more the introduction of cricket is yet another testament of British unintentionality.

The Indians took to the game as a means to take on their masters on a level playing field, and there is no ground more levelled than a cricket wicket. The game's greatest facet, though, has been its ability to unite the nation of India, and one can be sure that that was never what the Raj had in mind when they first drove stumps into Indian soil.

As the sociologist Ashis Nandy commented, *"Cricket is an Indian game, accidentally discovered by the British."* And as Tharoor conceded, *"A land divided by caste, creed, colour, culture, cuisine, custom and costume is united in consensus around a great conviction: cricket."*[1]

---

[1] THAROOR, Shashi, 'Cricket's Spiritual Home', *The Hindu online* (March 26, 2006)

CHAPTER
- XIV -

ON BALANCE

The 2014 YouGov poll carried out in the UK returned a 59% vote, stating the Empire was more something to be proud of than ashamed of. Perhaps there is imperial amnesia in Britain today. How does one explain such a result? Lack of education in imperial affairs? Indifference? Was the Empire really, on balance, a good thing? Or did the end justify the means?

The ordinary man in the street may have an excuse, he has a family to feed, and besides, he wasn't taught any of it at school. As for the academics, journalists, and documentary makers who have forged the public's perception of Empire, there can be no easy escape route for not having known any of this. And to fall to such depths of pointing fingers and claiming, *'well, they would have been worse had someone else ruled in our place'* is telling in its ambivalence.

That India speaks English, is the World's biggest democracy, writes in English and is taking up a significant role in the world economy is perhaps something the *British* should be more grateful for than India. And not just because they have saved Jaguar, Land Rover and the British railways by investing money and know-how in these industries.

India's improving situation does not in any way change the suffering of the past, where the least we can do in Britain today is not rub it in by saying we, who were never there, are *proud* of that racist, exacting regime.

So *'on balance'*, this author would argue, Britain's Indian venture gives a negative return as most positive achievements were more often the unintended by-product of financial self-interest. There are examples of good intentions, as we have seen, but they are not substantial enough to tip the balance in favour of Empire as a force for good.

India today does operate upon certain achievements put in place by the British, but the same could be said for every people that has been colonised down through the ages, taking on facets from their conquerors, unless you were unfortunate to have been conquered by Genghis Khan. Even Britain herself is no exception to this, having amalgamated many influences from the Romans, Vikings, Normans and even Dutch in the Glorious Revolution, to name but a few that have invaded her shores.

Progress is not a linear process and that concept, while clearly seen throughout history, is something many still struggle to comprehend and even resist to want to acknowledge. It is simply impossible for all people to improve at all times and to equal measures.

For those that argue that India should be grateful to Britain in anyway, could sum up this sense of 'debt' in the following anecdote of an anonymous Hindu speaking to an Englishman,

"You have taught us to fly in the air like birds, and to swim in the seas like fishes; but how to live on the earth you do not yet know."[1]

Perhaps, in truth, the reality is that it is not possible to say whether India benefitted from Britain on balance, for the simple reason that it is too early to tell. At a time while India is forging

---

[1] DURANT, p.101

a new sense of national identity, it is not expedient to credit anything to foreign occupation.

This would have been the case for Brittonic tribes with reference to their Roman occupiers, who not only subjugated them but also threw their island into anarchy on several occasions as their governor took the army with him to try his hand at becoming Emperor in Rome. To have persuaded Boudicca and her contemporaries that Rome was beneficial would have been a hard sell.

That is not the case today, if you ask a modern Briton about what Rome brought to Britannia. Ironically, Britain today is only aware of the pros and none of the cons. Likewise it is not an issue if you ask an Indian if Mughal rule benefitted India. That is an opinion that was internalised in the national and cultural discourse long ago.

And, of course, there is no more telling debate on empire than the scene from *The Life of Brian* where the People's Front of Judea weigh up the pros and cons of Roman rule. So from the Indian's perspective, 'What have the British ever done for us?'

In 2009, when Gordon Brown enjoyed his brief stint as Prime Minister, the government issued an unequivocal apology to Alan Turing, the mathematician responsible for breaking the Enigma codes that assisted in the final defeat of Nazi Germany. Turing took his own life, apparently, after being sentenced to chemical castration for *'gross indecency'*, in other words for having a sexual relationship with a man.

The apology came after Downing Street received a petition signed by 30,805 people, amongst whom were the novelist Ian

McEwan, the scientist Richard Dawkins and gay rights campaigner Peter Tatchell.

The apology and, even more so, the wording are of relevance here. Gordon Brown said, *"While Turing was dealt with under the law of the time and we can't put the clock back, his treatment was of course utterly unfair and I am pleased to have the chance to say how deeply sorry I and we all are for what happened to him."* He ends by saying, *"So on behalf of the British government, and all those who live freely thanks to Alan's work I am very proud to say: we're sorry, you deserved much better."*

It is therefore clear that the British government is capable of apologising, not once but twice in the same statement and that they are 'proud' to express such sentiment. It just seems unable, for the moment at least, to do the same thing where India is concerned.

Prime Minister David Cameron had a golden opportunity during his state visit to India when he went to Amritsar in 2013, but chose not to take it. Gordon Brown's apology referred to the year 1952, when Turing died, just nine years after the Bengal famine, and not so removed in time. If the government can apologise for wrong doing in the Fifties, it does not have to go far back to comment on the Forties, if it finds 1919 and Amritsar too removed.

The detractors will still insist that it is unnecessary, but there are continuous reminders that the need for a symbolic apology is vital to begin the re-educating process of a nation that does not know, or worse still thinks it knows, its imperial history.

This could not have been illustrated more clearly than when just days after the publication of Tharoor's book 'Inglorious Empire' the MP for North Somerset, Dr. Liam Fox, tweeted, *'The United Kingdom, is one of the few countries in the European Union that does not need to bury its Twentieth Century history.'* Dr. Fox played his hand close to his chest by selecting only the 20th century, as British India is much more than just the 47 years of British occupation in the 20th century.

However, even just the brief colonial period selected by Dr. Fox sees the Jallianwala Bagh massacre, a similar event in Dublin's Croke Park stadium when the RIC and Auxiliary Division fired into the sports fans, the Bengal famine of 1943 with 4.3 million dead, in part, due to British indifference and then came the brutal suppression of the Mau Mau rebellion in Kenya, which the government has already apologised for.

The worrying thing here is the fact that Dr. Fox is university educated, which does not exactly give British universities the sort of prestigious publicity they would wish for. But Tharoor has already told us that Britain is dolefully uneducated in matters of her Empire and Dr. Fox is plainly the latest reminder of that.

The year 2019 was the centenary of the Jallianwala Bagh massacre and the British government had to step forward and say something. Theresa May in parliament took time during Prime Minister's questions to comment on the massacre saying, *"We deeply regret what happened and the suffering caused,"* and that it was a, *"shameful scar on British history,"* but stopped short of an official apology. This contrasted with the leader of the Opposition, Jeremy Corbyn, who demanded a 'full and unequivocal apology.'

One may think that an apology is in order and no alternative explanation is possible, but spare a thought for what happened to Germany following the First World War and the burden of guilt that was heaped onto the nation. It didn't end well. If one is cornered into a situation where they are continually required to apologise for things in the past, it could have disastrous unforeseen outcomes that provoke the opposite effect and actually ignite pernicious nationalism. Added to that, all nations, all cultures and continents have things in their past that warrant apology.

Perhaps, acknowledgement is the best half-way house. After all, how can someone apologise for something they were not even alive to see, let alone participate in? If one becomes trapped by history they are doomed in the present. That said, an official apology could go a long way but it is necessary, always, to weigh up the potential pitfalls before choosing any course of action, especially one that could set a precedent.

Gordon Brown had been a minister when he said Britain should stop apologising for Empire, but was able to recognize wrong doing in the case of Turing. Why then could he not see any of the wrong doing of its Indian Empire, when there is plenty to consider? The wording is easy, the template already exists, it is a simple matter of substitution,

"While India was dealt with under the law of the time and we can't put the clock back, her treatment was of course utterly unfair and I am pleased to have the chance to say how deeply sorry I and we all are for what happened to her."

With today's technology all you need do then is press 'send', and then we can start focusing on the most important thing of all and that is start living the here and now so that we may better forge our future together.

Printed in Great Britain
by Amazon

32080874R00062